# FIRST JOHN

## Life at its Best

# FIRST JOHN

## Life at its Best

Roy L. Laurin

**KREGEL PUBLICATIONS**
Grand Rapids, Michigan 49501

*First John: Life at Its Best* by Roy L. Laurin. Published 1987 by Kregel Publications, a division of Kregel, Inc. All rights reserved.

**Library of Congress Cataloging-in-Publication Data**

Laurin, Roy L. (Roy Leonard), 1898-1966.
   First John: Life at Its Best.

   Reprint. Originally published: Epistle of John 3rd ed. Findlay, Ohio: Dunham Pub. Co., 1957.
   1. Bible.   N.T.   Epistles of John, 1st—Commentaries.
I. Title.
BS2805.3.L38        1987        227'.9406        86-27394
ISBN 0-8254-3136-0
4 5 6 7 8 Printing/Year 91 90 89 88 87

*Printed in the United States of America*

# CONTENTS

# FOREWORD

In stating leadership qualifications for the church through this age, the Spirit of God said,

"He gave some, evangelists; and some pastors and teachers."

The teacher has a real and divinely appointed place in the scheme of things today, and yet the gift of teaching, Bible teaching, seems to be comparatively rare.

The writer of this book has this gift to a marked degree. He not only has an analytical mind, but a synthetic grasp of the Bible as a whole, and of the Epistle here outlined. He also has the power to think clearly and to clothe his thoughts in solid, simple speech.

This book is commended not only for its fine spiritual message, but for its encouragement to Bible study. In fact a preacher might learn considerable concerning the art of exposition if he would carefully read and reread this volume. The greatest need of the church today is expository preaching. Apart from destructive liberalism, most of the church's weakness can be traced to the pulpit's proneness to topical and textual preaching. Let's have more messages along the line given in this book.

WILL H. HOUGHTON

# PREFACE

VERY early in my ministry I came to understand that the essential message of the Bible could be expressed by the single word, LIFE. The Bible's beginning tells of the creation of life while its ending tells of the perfection and consummation of life. Salvation is essentially the problem of obtaining life eternal. Christian experience is the expression of this new life which is found in Jesus Christ.

To whatever part of the Bible one may turn the direct or indirect reference of its subject matter is to life. This makes the interpretation of its message relatively simple as long as we understand this basic premise.

LIFE AT ITS BEST, first in the "Life" series, was written giving the general pattern for further volumes. It has therefore set the style in synthesis, analysis and presentation. It was not written in any sense as a critical or technical exposition but rather as a devotional exposition. Its expository technique is first to take apart the Word of God in terms of faith, truth and information and then put it back together again in terms of life, action and inspiration.

LIFE AT ITS BEST and the series of which it is a

part were written with both laymen and preachers in view, hence its language, style and homiletical treatment. It shows the anatomy of Scripture clothed with the beautiful garments of truth and sets forth its organic functions as it relates to conduct and service.

Roy L. Laurin

# INTRODUCTION

It is generally known that this letter of five chapters takes its name from John, one of the Twelve Apostles. He had a brother also among the twelve named James. Their family name was Zebedee and their mother was a very ambitious place-seeking person who had sought for her sons the chief places of the anticipated kingdom. Of the brothers, James was the first martyr among the twelve while John suffered a living death on the Isle of Patmos under the Roman Emperor Domitian.

If we consider the three Epistles of John as one (and we may properly do so) then John is seen to be the author of three Bible books, namely, the Gospel of John, the Epistle of John, and Revelation.

Although differing in many respects, the three bear marked similarities. They differ in the fact that one is history, one is doctrine and one is prophecy. They are alike in that they have a common characteristic, namely their emphasis upon the deity of Christ.

This emphasis is natural for one would expect that the man who was most intimate with Jesus knew the most about Him; and knowing the most about Him would write the highest truth concerning Him. John did this very thing.

There were three spheres of fellowship in the disciples' experience with Jesus. The first sphere included all twelve and it concerned service. The second sphere included three of the twelve, and it concerned the confidence and manifestations of an inner circle. The third sphere included one of the twelve, John, and concerned intimacies not enjoyed by any other. Out of this intimacy with Jesus came the knowledge of His person which made it possible for John to be the writer of three of the greatest books of the New Testament, all dealing with Jesus' divine person.

The Gospel of John is the deity of Jesus in life and death; the Epistle of John is the deity of Jesus in doctrine and experience; the Revelation of John is the unveiling of the deity of Jesus in eternal glory. The Gospel takes us back to the history of yesterday; the Epistle faces us with the practice of today; the Revelation carries us into the future unveiling of tomorrow's glory. All three, however, center their message in a common theme, the person of the divine Christ, which provides a symmetry and fullness in Scripture that should be another persuasion of its divine authorship as well as another encouragement to our faith.

There are other things common to this triad of writings.

In the Gospel there is life. In the Epistle there is love. In the Revelation there is light.

The Gospel is the work of a Narrator. The Epistle is the work of a Commentator. The Revelation is the work of a Revelator.

The Gospel goes back to the eternal past. The Epistle leads us to the life of the present. The Revelation unfolds the eternal future.

The Gospel was written that we "might believe that Jesus is the Christ, the Son of God." The Epistle was written "that your joy may be full." The Revelation was written that we might know "the things which shall be hereafter."

Knowing what John wrote we also have the reason why he wrote. There had come among the churches of his time a certain gross and destructive form of error. It originated with men known as gnostics who taught erroneous ideas concerning the person of Christ, denying that He had come in the flesh.

To be right concerning the person of Christ is vital, for if one is wrong here he is misled elsewhere. It is for this reason that this Epistle is most necessary today. We have modern teachers like these gnostics of John's time who teach false ideas concerning the person of Christ, possibly not denying so much that Jesus came in the *flesh,* but that Jesus came in *deity.* The false teachers of the first century said that Jesus was not man; the false teachers of the twentieth century say that Jesus is not God.

The particular error of the gnostics was concerning the person of Christ. To them Christ was only a divine being or "AEON"—a phantasm—who was joined with the human Jesus. This union, however, was not a literal incarnation, God coming in flesh, it was only an apparent or seeming union. The heavenly Christ did not in reality suffer and die; He left the human Jesus before He died on the cross. Thus ancient gnosticism denied that Christ came in the flesh, just as modern gnosticism denies that Christ came in deity by asserting that He was only a man. It was, and is, the most deadly teaching that Christianity has ever known. Avoid it as you would avoid a deadly poison.

We thank God that there is an answer for these things in the Scriptures. Every Bible believer can confidently face this modern world with a full assurance of faith in this Epistle. There is an emphatic answer to both ancientism and modernism in the three writings of John, the Gospel, the Epistle, and the Revelation. These were written within a very short time of each other. They were the last Scriptures written, John being the last of the inspired writers; therefore, they contain the last authentic testimony concerning Jesus Christ, His deity in history, in doctrine, and in prophecy.

While the devotional aspect of I John is our present concern, it was written as a doctrinal document rather than a devotional one. It was a prophylaxis for a church then endangered by ancient modernists. Besides, it was written to give assurance of personal salvation. "These things have I written unto you that believe on the name of the Son of God; that ye may know that ye have eternal life, and that ye may believe on the name of the Son of God" (5:13). In these words John declares the reason for his writing and since it is a declared reason we should consider it a personal challenge to our Christian experience. Do we think or do we know? Do we hope or do we affirm? A faithful inquiry into this latter will bring an earnest soul into a knowing experience. The Epistle had no specific and immediate destination as in the case of other New Testament Epistles. It was the informal address of a Christian father to members of his family who were scattered beyond his personal reach.

It is a reminder that the peril which was general to all Christians of that day is likewise general to all Christians of our day. It should be read as though it was written immediately to us since it concerns spiritual problems which immediately concern us.

The Epistle sets forth two great and related facts of Christian experience, namely, life and love. Life is the beginning of Christian experience and love is the end of Christian experience. Life is its cause and love is its effect. Life is its generation and love its manifestation.

With this in mind we will be prepared to find "Life at Its Best" because it is a life of love.

There is lack of structure in this letter to such an evident extent that it does not lend itself to a well-defined or easy chapter division. A clue to a convenient division is found in the three opening verses where the life of God was made known or manifested that it might result in eternal life for us. In the five chapters we find at least twelve different characteristics of "Life at Its Best."

1. The Manifested Life — I John 1:1-4
2. The Illuminated Life — I John 1:5-2:2
3. The True Life — I John 2:3-11
4. The Abiding Life — I John 2:12-17
5. The False Life — I John 2:18-27
6. The Coming Life — I John 2:28-3:3
7. The Conquering Life — I John 3:4-10
8. The Love Life — I John 3:11-24
9. The Discerning Life — I John 4:1-6
10. The Love Life Emphasized — I John 4:7-21
11. The Overcoming Life — I John 5:1-12
12. The Eternal Life — I John 5:13-21

# OUTLINE OF FIRST JOHN

A. THE MANIFESTED LIFE. I John 1:1-4.
    I. THE BEGINNING OF LIFE. Verse 1.
    II. THE EXPERIENCE OF LIFE. Verse 2.
    III. THE FELLOWSHIP OF LIFE. Verse 3.
    IV. THE JOY OF LIFE. Verse 4.

B. THE ILLUMINATED LIFE. I JOHN 1:5-2:2.
    I. THE CHRISTIAN MESSAGE OF LIGHT. Verse 5.
    II. THE CHRISTIAN MANNER OF LIFE.
        Verses 6-2:2.
        1. First Fault and Its Correction. Verses 6, 7.
        2. Second Fault and Its Correction.
          Verses 8, 9.
        3. Third Fault and Its Correction.
          Verses 10-2:2.

C. THE TRUE LIFE. I John 2:3-11.
    I. MAN'S MEASUREMENT.
    II. GOD'S MEASUREMENT.
        1. Keeping. Verses 3-5.
        2. Walking. Verses 6, 7.
        3. Loving. Verses 8-11

D. THE ABIDING LIFE. I John 2:12-17.
    I. THE DIFFERENT KINDS OF CHRISTIANS.
        Verses 12-14.

     II. THE WRONG KIND OF LOVE. Verses 15, 16.

     III. THE RIGHT KIND OF LIFE. Verse 17.

E. THE FALSE LIFE. I John 2:18-27.

     I. THE AGE. Verse 18a.

     II. THE CHARACTERISTIC OF THE AGE.
        Verses 18b, 19.

     III. THE SAFEGUARDS OF THE SOUL IN THIS AGE.
        Verses 20-27.

       1. The Spirit of God. Verse 20.

       2. The Word of God. Verse 24.

       3. The Life of God. Verse 25.

F. THE COMING LIFE. I John 2:28-3:3.

     I. HIS COMING AND OUR CONFIDENCE.
        Verse 28.

     II. HIS COMING AND OUR NEW BIRTH. Verse 29.

     III. HIS COMING AND OUR NAME. 3:1.

     IV. HIS COMING AND OUR CHANGE. Verse 2.

     V. HIS COMING AND OUR ATTITUDE. Verse 3.

G. THE CONQUERING LIFE. I John 3:4-10.

     I. TO SIN IS UNLAWFUL. Verse 4.

     II. TO SIN IS UNREASONABLE. Verse 5.

     III. TO SIN IS UNSPIRITUAL. Verses 6-8.

     IV. TO SIN IS UNCHRISTIAN. Verses 9, 10.

H. THE LOVE LIFE. I John 3:11-24.

     I. LOVE PROVES OUR UNLIKENESS TO HUMAN
       NATURE. Verses 11, 12.

     II. LOVE PROVES OUR UNLIKENESS TO THE
       WORLD. Verse 13.

     III. LOVE PROVES OUR NEW LIKENESS TO CHRIST.
       Verses 14, 15.

IV. Love Proves Our New Likeness to God.
    Verses 16, 17.

V. Love Proves Our New Likeness to the
    Truth. Verses 18-24.

    1. The Assurance of the Truth. Verse 19.
    2. The Assurance of an Uncondemning
       Heart. Verses 20, 21.
    3. The Assurance of Answers to Prayer.
       Verses 22-24.

I. THE DISCERNING LIFE. I John 4:1-6.

    I. By the Indwelling of a Divine Spirit.
       Verse 1.

    II. By the Confession of a Divine Lord.
       Verses 2, 3.

    III. By the Presence of a Divine Life. Verse 4.

    IV. By the Authority of a Divine Word.
       Verses 5, 6.

J. THE LOVE LIFE EMPHASIZED. I John 4:7-21.

    I. Love is the Essence of God. Verses 7,8.

    II. Love Found its Highest Manifestation in
       Christ. Verses 9-11.

    1. The Purpose of Love. Verse 9.
    2. The Priority of Love. Verse 10.
    3. The Product of Love. Verse 11.

    III. Love is the Certain Evidence of the New
       Birth. Verses 12-16.

    IV. Love Brings Boldness Before Judgment.
       Verse 17.

    V. Love Banishes Fear. Verse 18.

    VI. Love Verifies Love. Verses 19, 20.

VII. Love Fulfills God's Commandment.
    Verse 21.

K. THE OVERCOMING LIFE. I John 5:1-12.
    I. Love and Life. Verses 1-3.
    II. Faith and Victory. Verses 4, 5.
    III. Christ and Witnesses. Verses 6-12.
        1. Christ and His Witnesses. Verses 6-9.
            (1) *In heaven.* Verse 7.
            (2) *In earth.* Verse 8.
        2. The Christian and His Witness.
            Verses 10-12.

L. THE ETERNAL LIFE. I John 5:13-21.
    I. The Assurance of the Possession of
        Eternal Life. Verse 13.
        1. Because of a Settled Sin Question. 1:7-10.
        2. Because We Keep His Commandments.
            2:4, 5.
        3. Because There Is Love. 3:14.
        4. Because of the Witness of the Holy Spirit.
            3:24.
        5. Because of the Word of God. 5:1.
    II. The Assurance of the Power of Prayer.
        Verses 14, 15.
    III. The Assurance of the Protection against
        Sin. Verses 16, 17.
    IV. The Assurance of the Presence of Christ.
        Verses 18-21.
        1. The Christian's New Ability. Verse 18.
        2. The Christian's New Identity. Verse 19.
        3. The Christian's New Knowledge. Verse 20.

# 1

## THE MANIFESTED LIFE

### 1:1-4

LIFE is presented in terms of a person. It is not an abstract theory set forth in theological and philosophical ideas. It is something tangible and real. This life is the life of God manifested in His Son Jesus Christ and brought down to our level in flesh and blood.

I. THE BEGINNING OF LIFE. Verse 1.

> "That which was from the beginning, which we have heard, which we have seen with our eyes, which we have looked upon, and our hands have handled, of the Word of life."

The opening phrase "That which was from the beginning" brings to our attention something more than the immediate matters confronting these and all other Christians. It overshadows the present with a past. It reminds us that the child of God is not a subject of circumstances but a child of destiny whose origin goes back to a beginning. It starts where everything that is important must start, at a beginning. It is at the beginning that one starts his reading of a book. It is at the beginning that one learns the alphabet. It is at the beginning that one must learn how to live.

The beginning of Christian experience is not the twentieth century, but the first century; it is not the catechism but the Cross; it is not baptism but the new birth; it is not a new leaf but a new life. This personal beginning is based on the historical beginning to which this text refers.

There are three beginnings mentioned in the Scriptures.

1. The Beginning of Genesis 1:1. "In the beginning God created the heaven and the earth." This refers to the beginning of the universe which we commonly mistake as the beginning of man. The Bible does not say what is the date of this beginning but it antedates man's appearance. It was the beginning of matter from which proceeds the creative operations of God that resulted in the world and all its parts.

2. The Beginning of John 1:1. "In the beginning was the Word, and the Word was with God, and the Word was God." This refers to what may properly be termed the unbegun beginning. It was the beginning before the beginning. It was the beginning which began the beginning. We speak facetiously of beginning to commence but this is the beginning which commenced all things.

3. The Beginning of I John 1:1. "That which was from the beginning, which we have heard, which we have seen with our eyes, which we have looked

upon, and our hands have handled, of the Word of life." This refers to the most recent of the beginnings. It is the beginning of Christian experience. Christianity dates with Christ and Christ dates with God. In fact, Christ is as dateless as God. The source of our spiritual life is the same as the source of our natural life. Both go back to God. One goes back to the Cross and the other goes back to Creation. The Cross is the correction of the curse upon life which came with the entrance of sin after Creation.

Here is the starting place of faith and experience for the Christian. Even our calendar years and days begin at this point. How much more important then that we recognize it as the beginning of our new destiny.

Some time ago the German Nazis asserted that all Christian symbols were to be eliminated from the history books used in German schools. Instead of dates like 397 B.C. and A.D. 1939 Nazi school books refer to 397 V.ZTR meaning before time computed, and 1939 N.ZTR meaning after time computed.

In seeking to eliminate Christ from daily life the Nazis acted like others before them who "did not like to retain God in their knowledge." Nevertheless, in this effort they must still acknowledge that the computation of all time is from Christ. All time before the coming of Jesus Christ points toward His arrival and all time since, points back upon it. He is the eternal I Am, the central figure of time and eternity. He is our new beginning. With Him commences our experience with God. From Him dates every divine attempt to bless the human race. Without Him there may be religious efforts and experiences but there can neither be redemption nor Christian experience.

In this manner all the events of this Epistle are dated and all the experiences of the Christian are founded. They have an historical setting. They have a definite meaning. They cannot mean anything we may desire to think of, but something so definite and evident that we can point to their beginning and say, this is what Christianity means.

Reduced to a single, simple phrase it is this—"the Word of Life." Jesus Christ is the "Word of Life" while the Bible is the "Word of Truth." The "Word of Life" is God's word in flesh while the "Word of Truth" is God's word in writing. In Christ God clothed Himself in flesh while in the Bible God clothed Himself in words. In Christ God speaks by a life while in the Bible God speaks by the letter.

This "Word of Life" who is Christ, is real and demonstrable. He is not an abstraction but a demonstration. He is a real person who lived in real life at a real time in history. Being God, He was also man.

What John is saying about Christ was a refutation of what the gnostics had said. They denied His actual and physical manhood. They contended that He was a phantom. This John could deny for he and his colleagues had verified the reality of Christ's humanity by the testimony of ears, eyes and hands.

They had heard, they had seen and they had handled Christ. Christ was manifest to their senses as He is now manifest to our spirits. He is now a spiritual reality as once He was a physical reality.

When John tells us in one instance that Jesus Christ has been "seen with our eyes" and in another instance that he has "looked upon" Him, he is not wasting words. It is amplification rather than duplication. When he says "which we have looked upon" he refers to something more than an optical perception. This is a spiritual apperception. This is to gaze so intently and deeply as to come to a true knowledge of Jesus Christ.

Here were men who had heard Him, seen Him and touched Him. They had tested their experience of Christ by so many evidences that they could not have been mistaken. They knew He was a real man and not some vision or illusion.

Christ was God. God did not merely appear in Christ in godlike qualities. It was upon this manifestation of God that John looked when he saw Jesus.

As gnosticism denied that Jesus came physically, so modern unbelief denies that Jesus lives personally in the lives of men today. To this our answer is the same: not argument but experience. To be sure, we do not see, hear and feel Him with our physical senses; but we have confirmed Him by the faculties of our spiritual senses and can say, "Whom having not seen, ye love; in whom, though now ye see him not, yet believing, ye rejoice with joy unspeakable and full of glory" (I Pet. 1:8).

No one of us should forget the solemn fact that there comes a time in the life and experience of every person when God is in his hands. It is the reverse of the usual conception of man in the hands of God. That is always true, but it is equally true that God in Christ is in our hands. We must pass judgment upon Him. We must either affirm that He is the Son of God and accept Him as Saviour, or we must deny Him as such. In our denial He becomes but a mere man incapable of working the works of God for us. It is indeed a solemn matter to pass judgment on Jesus Christ.

What happened in the first century was not a reduction of deity to humanity as if Jesus was only a man. It was, instead, a manifestation of the mystery of deity in human flesh. God made Himself manifest in Christ. We sign manifests in which we make declarations of possession. A manifest in business terms is a list or invoice of a ship's cargo to be exhibited at the customhouse. Once, upon returning from Honolulu, it was necessary for us to sign a manifest concerning the possession of fruit. Because of a rigid embargo on the importation of all fruit from the Islands, we were required to make this declaration a day or two out of our mainland port.

Christ is God's manifest. He is the declaration of the unseen qualities of God's character and nature. He is the exhibition of divine love. He is the revelation of the divine purpose for man. In this respect He is not a mere sample of God; not a phantom; not an idea, but God Himself. This, then, is the manifestation which is Christ.

II. THE EXPERIENCE OF LIFE. Verse 2.

"(For the life was manifested, and we have seen it, and bear witness, and shew unto you that eternal life, which was with the Father, and was manifested unto us)."

Christianity has its theoretical explanation but it is more than a theory of religion; it is an experience of life. It must be to us what it was to the apostles. It must be Someone we experience. It must be a thing so definite that we can bear witness to it. It must be the experience of a God who walks with us and not merely a God who lives in a temple whom we must go and worship. It must be a reality.

When a certain minister asked why motion pictures take such a hold upon the public while churches become depleted, a prominent motion picture executive replied: "We take the unreal and impossible and make them real, w h e r e a s the present day preacher makes the real, though seemingly impossible, unreal." This diagnosis seems to be quite generally true. We fail to exploit the reality of our faith. It is held up in some doctrine or theory and consequently held in by the mind so that it cannot reach our hands for service, our feet for walking and our face for reflection.

It sounds good to talk about the pageantry, the beauty and the mystery of worshiping God. It appeals to some when Christianity is wrapped in beautiful vestments and displayed in spectacular parades and elaborate ceremonies, but all such is out of date. There was a time for the mystery; but that time is not now, for we live in the days of the manifestation. God has unveiled Himself in the Nazarene. With His own hands He tore the temple veil in twain. The sacrifice, the Levitical priesthood, the ceremony, the physical splendor are all gone. The mystery is past and the manifestation has come. It is no longer God in a temple of gold and stone, but God in that temple which is our body.

The manifestation of Christ was His incarnation. The experience of Christ is our regeneration. The incarnation meant God in Christ. The regeneration means God in man. Manifestation means magnification.

The gnostics of the first century attempted to exclude Christ from experience and to keep Him at a respectable religious d i s t a n c e. It is similarly attempted today. They were refuted by the experience of those who saw and handled the One who manifested God. Their modern counterparts may likewise be refuted by our experience and our display of the reality of Christ. Christianity has its arguments but it also has its witnesses. It will stand trial in any court of investigation.

That which these witnesses experienced was not

a passing emotional reaction. It is described as being "eternal life." It was not something which vanished in a moment or a day. It was not something which lasted for a lifetime. It was forever. For this they did not have to wait until death. There was no doubting and no questioning. It was bold assurance for eternal life is something to have and to know you have it, now. It was known in the first century. It may be known in the twentieth century.

## III. THE FELLOWSHIP OF LIFE. Verse 3.

"That which we have seen and heard declare we unto you, that ye also may have fellowship with us: and truly our fellowship is with the Father, and with his Son Jesus Christ."

Fellowship is much more than companionship or comradeship. It means community of thought and interest. It means a state of unity and harmony. It implies what was true in the Garden of Eden when man's experience of God was intimate and immediate. It is a mutual "entering into" of one another's experience. This original state of man's relation to God is restored by Christian experience. It is to be found in fellowship.

There are two phases of fellowship.

1. Fellowship with Others.

This is described by the words: "that ye also may have fellowship with us." This means that we are at one with each other. It means sharing our common experience of eternal life. When we exchange what we know of Christ we are having fellowship. This can be the most enriching experience of life, producing a bond of affection more endearing than blood relationship. It will create a more intimate understanding than can be produced by family ties because its basis is a new life and a new Lord. It amplifies and intensifies life so that we find it more enjoyable than could otherwise be true.

2. Fellowship with God.

This is described by the words: "truly our fellowship is with the Father, and with his Son Jesus Christ."

We can only have fellowship with God in Jesus Christ. He alone makes this experience possible. God is reconciling the world to Himself in Christ and only by our identity to Jesus Christ by faith can we be reconciled to God and have this fellowship. Outside of Christ we have a creature identity with God. In Christ we have a Christian identity with God which means that we are a member of the divine family and a subject of the divine kingdom. This alone makes fellowship with God possible, and fellowship with God is the only thing that makes fellowship with others possible. Human fellowship has a divine basis. When we think rightly of Him we will think rightly of others. When we live rightly with Him we will live rightly with others.

Narrow-minded people dreadfully abuse the word "fellowship," making it mean a sectarian fellowship. They disdainfully speak of other Christians not belonging to "our fellowship." My friends, Christian fellowship is not the fellowship of one denomination, one sect, one clique of some secluded few who think that they have a corner on divine truth. It is a divine fellowship "with the Father and with his Son Jesus Christ." It is as wide as deity, but as narrow as the strait gate and the narrow way.

We must not forget that *fellowship* begins with *experience.* There is much being said and written these days about being in harmony with God. Our bookstores are filled with philosophies of harmony. Our pulpits and classrooms offer methods of harmony with God by *what we think.* Such a harmony is an ethical salvation and is not new, being the same as ancient gnosticism, which said that salvation was not a saving from iniquity but a salvation from ignorance. It is not unlike the modern ethical salvation which teaches that we are not saved from sin but from unkind, uncharitable thinking.

Other intellectuals say that we can establish harmony with God by *what we* do. This is a moralistic salvation, one from effects and not causes. Still others affirm that we can establish harmony with God by *keeping the Law.* This is a legalistic salvation, and is one from conscience and not nature.

The Scriptures declare that we can establish harmony with God only by *what we are,* that we can have fellowship with God only when we become like Him. This is only possible through another birth, the new birth of regeneration in which we become "partakers of the divine nature." Regeneration is a change of nature which in turn means a change in thought, word and deed.

Let us guard and cherish this "fellowship" against rupture, against suspicion, jealousy, selfishness, and disloyalty. Let past tragedies of broken fellowship be lessons of grace never to occur again, serving only to lift us to higher experiences.

The day may be nearer than we expect when these ties of fellowship will be the last line of defense against the encroachments of liberty as we approach the increase of antichristianity. It is then that the common bond of Christian fellowship will sustain us.

IV. The Joy of Life. Verse 4.

"And these things write we unto you, that your joy may be full."

This is one of the purposes for which this Epistle was written. It was written in order "that your joy may be full."

As fellowship is the result of experience so joy is the result of fellowship. It is not said to have its source in riches although riches do afford no small measure of comfort and satisfaction. It is not said to have its source in pleasure although pleasure may bring diversion and recreation. Joy is mentioned in connection with Christ because it has its source in character. Joy is born, not bought. It is the cause of our happiness, not the effect of our pleasure.

The fullness of our joy will come from our experience and knowledge of "these things" which are a matter of record in this Epistle. It will not come from a mere frame of mind but rather from the shape of life and the state of heart. It will not result from circumstances, nor conversely, will circumstances rob us of joy. "These things" which form the source of a full and continuing joy are an experience of life in Christ and a fellowship of life in Christ and with one another. Here is a reasonable philosophy and a tangible recipe for life. Here is something practical.

# 2

## THE ILLUMINATED LIFE

### 1:5-2:2

EVERY provision of God has a reason and a purpose. When it gives us a revelation of God as light it is for the purpose of illumination. The reason for the illumination is found in the fact that a natural life is lived in darkness. God is light for such darkness. Darkness is the result of sin and sin constitutes the greatest human problem. Many are unwilling to recognize this, yet it is true. Every difficulty in the world goes back to this basic cause. For this reason the message of the Bible is not primarily a literary one, or a religious one, or an historical one, but a spiritual one. It focuses light on our darkness. It deals with our sin.

Sin is something more than a creature problem. It is a family problem as well. We do not face its penalty but its power. The power of sin can be operative in the life of a Christian as well as a non-Christian. This problem is faced and dealt with now.

I. THE CHRISTIAN MESSAGE OF LIGHT. Verse 5.

"This then is the message which we have heard of him, and declare unto you, that God is light, and in him is no darkness at all."

This light which God is, is primarily directed to the Christian's sin problem. God is light for all darkness, but its connection here is with the spiritual darkness in which a child of God may walk when and if he is out of fellowship with God.

The source of illumination which brings this light is twofold: first, the Word of Truth which is the Scriptures and second, the Word of Life which is Christ of whom this is said, "For God, who commanded the light to shine out of darkness, hath shined in our hearts, to give the light of the knowledge of the glory of God in the face of Jesus Christ" (II Cor. 4:6).

The fact that this message of light comes in the sequence it does, following the believers experience of life, has significance in connection with the three beginnings to which reference has already been made.

The first beginning of Genesis 1 presents the picture of an earth where darkness is universal. This darkness was material. The first creative act of God was to bring light into the midst of this primeval darkness.

The second beginning of John 1 deals with the pre-beginning of Genesis 1. It goes back of creation to the Creator. It results ultimately in the Creator becoming the Redeemer. The God of the beginning becomes the Christ of the new beginning. It speaks of a moral darkness in man which is as universal as the material darkness of the world in the first begin-

ning. In Genesis we have the history of creation
while in John we have the history of re-creation. In
Genesis we find disorganized matter while in John
we have disordered man. To this state of moral affairs God brings light, for in speaking of the Word
which became "flesh and dwelt among us" it says,
"In him was life; and the life was the light of men.
And the light shineth in darkness."

The third beginning of I John reveals another kind
of darkness. Here it is neither material nor moral,
but spiritual darkness. It is not darkness in the physical sphere, nor darkness in the sinner's sphere, but
darkness in the Christian's sphere. This is a message
primarily to believers. The saint has a sin problem
as well as the sinner. The sinner's sin problem is one
of justification while the saint's sin problem is one
of sanctification. To this problem, as in the previous
cases, God brings light, "This then is the message
.  .  .  that God is light." In the Epistle of John
God is light for the walk of the believer.

The Bible speaks of darkness in a number of different phases. There is *material darkness*. "And the
earth was without form, and void; and darkness was
upon the face of the deep. And the Spirit of God
moved upon the face of the waters" (Gen. 1:2). This
is the darkness which preceded the original beginning.

There is *natural darkness*. "Because that, when
they knew God, they glorified him not as God, neither were thankful; but became vain in their imagin-

ations, and their foolish heart was darkened" (Rom. 1:21). This is the darkness into which all men are born and refers to a condition of character which is alien to God. In this darkness it is natural for children to be untruthful, dishonest, disobedient and temperamental. No child ever needs to be taught how to lie or cheat or to disobey or to display temper. Instead he needs correction, control and discipline. This condition is natural to all men and it points to an inherited quality of life.

It was recently reported in the *Scientific World* that "Some scientists, trying to discover what causes hereditary insanity, believe that we all come into the world with 'inherited morals.'

"The Bureau of Human Heredity, in London, which is organizing a world-wide research to determine what effect ancestry has on human character and life, announces—'we were born, not made. Our mental, moral and physical makeup is decided for us before birth. Conscience is inborn. Some people are color-blind to right and wrong, just as others cannot distinguish between red and green. No amount of cultivation will turn a thistle into an orchid. The same rules apply to human beings.' "

There is *mental darkness*. "Having the understanding darkened, being alienated from the life of God through the ignorance that is in them, because of the blindness of their heart" (Eph. 4:18). This very definitely qualifies the normal thinking of all men. Man may be capable of scientific and philosophic thinking to a very productive degree, but in spiritual thinking and the knowledge of God he is definitely limited.

There is *prophetic darkness.* "A day of darkness and of gloominess, a day of clouds and of thick darkness, as the morning spread upon the mountains: a great people and a strong; there hath not been ever the like, neither shall be any more after it, even to the years of many generations" (Joel 2:2). This darkness will plunge the world into a state of vast and universal confusion.

There is *supernatural darkness.* "For we wrestle not against flesh and blood, but against principalities, against powers, against the rulers of the darkness of this world, against spiritual wickedness in high places" (Eph. 6:12). This is the darkness of evil spirits headed by that great spirit personality who is Satan. It is in the occult world but its influence on us is as real as the influence of gravity.

There is *eternal darkness.* "Raging waves of the sea, foaming out their own shame; wandering stars, to whom is reserved the blackness of darkness forever" (Jude 13). This is darkness that is endless. It is without alteration or correction.

There is *spiritual darkness.* "This then is the message which we have heard of him, and declare unto you, that God is light, and in him is no darkness at all" (I John 1:5). This is the darkness that comes when a believer is out of fellowship with God. It is for this darkness that God becomes our light. When we walk in the light there is fellowship which means joy and righteousness. When we are not walking in the light there is no fellowship but a susceptibility to sin. It is for this problem of sin in a Christian's walk that this message of John is primarily given. It holds the prospect of much profit and blessing to all who will understand and heed its teaching.

II. THE CHRISTIAN MANNER OF LIFE. Verses 6-2:2.

Three times the three words "if we say" occur to determine and outline the teaching of this section. In each case they occur in even-numbered verses and are followed by odd-numbered verses which give the correction of the fault and the remedy for the trouble.

For example in verse 6 it is "If we say that we have fellowship with him, and walk in darkness, we lie, and do not the truth." Then in verse 7 there is the correction of the fault, "But if we walk in the light, as he is in the light, we have fellowship one with another, and the blood of Jesus Christ his Son cleanseth us from all sin." Here then is a fault and its correction, all within the Christian's sphere of life. There are three such faults and their corrections.

### 1. The First Fault and Its Correction.

"If we say that we have fellowship with him, and walk in darkness, we lie, and do not the truth: But if we walk in the light, as he is in the light, we have fellowship one with another, and the blood of Jesus Christ his Son cleanseth us from all sin" (verses 6,7).

The person in view is a believer. This creates the hypothetical and possible case of a believer saying he has fellowship with God, but yet is walking in spiritual darkness. Such a person lies, for it is impossible to be in God's fellowship and in spiritual darkness at the same time.

Spiritual darkness may be defined in three ways.

(1) *It is our walk outside the Word of God.* "He that saith, I know him, and keepeth not his commandments, is a liar, and the truth is not in him" (I John 2:4).

(2) *It is our walk outside the way of God.*" I am the way, the truth, and the life: no man cometh unto the Father, but by me" (John 14:6).

(3) *It is our walk outside the will of God.* "Be ye not unequally yoked together with unbelievers: for what fellowship hath righteousness with unrighteousness? and what communion hath light with darkness? And what concord hath Christ with Belial? or what part hath he that believeth with an infidel? And what agreement hath the temple of God with idols? for ye are the temple of the living God; as God hath said, I will dwell in them, and walk in them; and I will be their God, and they shall be my people. Wherefore come out from among them, and be ye separate, saith the Lord, and touch not the unclean thing, and I will receive you" (II Cor. 6:14-17).

The first act of the Creator in the creative beginning was illumination. The second act was division.

After creating light He "divided the light from the darkness." Light and darkness, day and night are two separate and distinct spheres of existence.

When Jesus Christ came to be the Light of the world the effect was similar. First there was the illumination of man, then there was the division of the illuminated from the unilluminated. He divided His disciples from the rest of the world. His Church became a called-out people. Their way became a different way and their walk a different walk.

It was to this division that He referred when He said, "I am come to set a man at variance (divided into two parts) against his father, and the daughter against her mother, and the daughter-in-law against her mother-in-law. And a man's foes shall be they of his own household" (Matt. 10:35,36).

Darkness was not created. It is the absence of light. It has always existed and exists now where the light is absent. The recession of the sun across the horizon draws darkness in its wake. Just so darkness in our lives can only come by the recession of Christ through our refusal to respect the divisions He has made between light and darkness by the Word of God, the way of God and the will of God.

The proof of the reality of our fellowship is not in our words, but in our walk, for its says, "If we walk in the light, as he is in the light, we have fellowship one with another, and the blood of Jesus Christ his Son cleanseth us from all sin."

This supplies the correction for the fault. It is both

a correction for sin and a preventive of sin. It is not how we walk, in the sense of being faultless and perfect, but where we walk. It is our walk in the Light which produces the effect described.

There is a double effect resulting from walking in the Light.

a. Fellowship—"We have fellowship one with another."

Light has a socializing effect. It attracts and generates. Wherever you find light you will find people. Well lighted places always draw crowds. When we walk in God's light it will create an atmosphere of fellowship to which people will be attracted. Light is divisive only where darkness is concerned. Among Christians who walk in it, it is unifying. Divisions among Christians never occur in the light. They can only come from darkness. The light generates fellowship and fellowship means unity, harmony and understanding. A common paternity will lead to a common fraternity.

b. Cleansing—"And the blood of Jesus Christ his Son cleanseth us from all sin."

Light has a sanctifying effect. As we walk in it the blood of Christ becomes efficacious for all of sin's pollutions. This is the cleansing of sanctification. A sinner's cleansing from sin is in justification. A believer's cleansing from sin is in sanctification. It is preventive as well as corrective for as we walk in the Light Christ's death-blood becomes our life-blood and brings us cleansing from sin before it can be brought forth into words and deeds.

Through the ancient city of Damascus there flowed a river whose source was from the rock-foundations which underlay it. It served a double purpose. At its source it provided clean water for the city's life. In its course through the city it provided cleansing for the city's pollutions. By its constant flow the city was kept clean. Similarly, as we walk in the light we are kept clean from life's pollutions.

We should carefully notice that it is in the light that the blood of Christ is efficacious. God is light and God is revealed both in the word of truth which is the Bible and in the word of life which is Jesus Christ. As we walk in both these sources of light, the blood of cleansing is efficacious for the daily pollutions of our walk through life.

### 2. The Second Fault and Its Correction.

"If we say that we have no sin, we deceive ourselves, and the truth is not in us. If we confess our sins, he is faithful and just to forgive us our sins, and to cleanse us from all unrighteousness" (Verses 8,9).

It was common for the gnostic teachers to say they had no sin. This was an evidence of ignorance and self-deception. Moreover, it was willful ignorance and self-deception.

Today we have good people saying the same thing in another way. To them there is no sin if it is a mistake of the head. It can only be sinful when it is a mistake of the heart; that is, something intentional, deliberate and willful. This is sophistry and self-deception. There can be no arbitrary distinctions made in the matter of sin. Whether it is a mental mistake or a spiritual mistake, intentional or unintentional, it is sin.

To claim present sinlessness because of personal perfection is to deceive ourselves. We certainly do not deceive our relatives, friends or neighbors and what is more certain, we do not deceive God.

In claiming sinlessness Bible truth is not involved. It is personal truth. It is "the truth" as a principle of life that "is not in us." We are not faithful to ourself when we make such a claim. We are not accurate in reporting our own state.

The correction of this fault follows in the statement of the next verse, "If we confess our sins, he is faithful and just to forgive us our sins, and to cleanse us from all unrighteousness." Here are three great spiritual facts.

(1) *The confession of sins.*

The subject of our confession is our sins which must include anything of a conscious or unconscious character, both of commission and omission. The confession is to be made directly to Jesus Christ without the necessity of an intermediate advocate. We need neither friendly nor priestly helpers in the confession of sin. It is a personal matter before a personal Christ.

(2) *The forgiveness of sins.*

Forgiveness is conditional. It requires confession. Unconfessed sin in a believer will bring the loss of fellowship, but it cannot bring the loss of salvation. Unconfessed sin will remain until the Judgment Seat of Christ where it will be dealt with; not as a judicial thing resulting in the loss of life, but as a spiritual thing resulting in the loss of reward.

(3) *The cleansing of sins.*

These three facts concerning sin in a believer are interlocking and inter-related. Sin can never be cleansed from us until it is forgiven in us and it is never forgiven in us unless it has been confessed by us. Confession is our responsibility while forgiveness and cleansing are God's. No act of ours can produce either forgiveness or cleansing. It can only come from the grace of God. Confession upon our part is the fulfillment of a condition which makes it possible for grace to operate.

Since two cleansings are mentioned here it is interesting to notice the contrast they present.

*There is cleansing from sin by walking in verse 7.*

This is an unconscious cleansing since walking is an unconscious and involuntary action. One does not need to think in order to walk. It is one of those automatic functions performed by the body such as breathing. As one walks in the Light he is kept cleansed from all sin. It is a spiritual prophylactic.

*There is the cleansing from sins by confessing in verse 9.* This is a conscious cleansing. In the cleansing by walking we obtain cleansing as we walk. In this cleansing by confessing we obtain cleansing only when we confess. The first cleansing is from the principle of sin. The second cleansing is from the practice of sins.

A further contrast is found in the fact that in the first cleansing it says, "the blood of Jesus Christ his Son cleanseth us from all sin" while in the second cleansing it says, "he is faithful and just to forgive us our sins and cleanse us from all unrighteousness." In one case it is the blood of Christ, in the other case it is the faithfulness and justice of Christ. One is the means and the other is the ground of forgiveness and cleansing.

Evan Hopkins, a seeker after God, reasoned like this concerning sin and cleansing:

He turned to the Bible and opened it at I John 1:9. "If we confess our sins, he is faithful and just to forgive us our sins, and to cleanse us from all unrighteousness." The Spirit of God enabled him to see what was implied in those words, the idea of a covenant. And he asked himself the question:

"If we confess our sins, God is faithful and just. Faithful to whom? Just to what?"

He thought there must be behind those words a covenant, and the whole truth flashed through his mind.

"There is a covenant," he said, "between the Father and the Son. God has obligated Himself to accept, forgive, and save every soul that comes to Him through Jesus Christ. Jesus has paid the sinner's penalty; He has died in the sinner's place; He has suffered in the sinner's stead. Therefore the debt has been paid. God must be faithful in the forgiveness of sin, and He is just in so doing because Christ has met every claim."

Evan Hopkins knelt down and prayed something like this, "Lord, for Jesus sake, because of what He has done in fulfillment of that everlasting covenant, accept, forgive, and save me."

### 3. The Third Fault and Its Correction.

"If we say that we have not sinned, we make him a liar, and his word is not in us. My little children, these things write I unto you, that ye sin not. And if any man sin, we have an advocate with the Father, Jesus Christ the righteous: And he is the propitiation for our sins: and not for ours only, but also for the sins of the whole world" (I John 1:10-2:1, 2.)

The reference is still to Christians but the application may be more extensive. Anyone claiming, as in verse 8, that he has no sin in the present makes himself an untruthful person because he is not honestly reporting what his conscience is saying. Anyone claiming, as in verse 10, that he has not sinned in the past, makes God an untruthful person because God's word speaks of sin in both believer and non-believer. So far as the non-believer is concerned, there are such statements as Romans 3:23: "For all have sinned and come short of the glory of God." Anyone denying this opposes the veracity of God.

The first denial of sin, as in verse 8, is of sin as an activity. The second denial of sin, as in verse 10, is of sin as a state. Both the activity and the state are existent in the Christian sphere. The difference lies in this, that sin in an unbeliever will bear its judicial consequence of death. In a believer it will receive forgiveness and cleansing upon confession or else it will remain for adjudication at the Judgment Seat of Christ where its adjustment will be in the form of loss rather than judicial penalty. As in the case of the law of our land as stated in the Bill of Rights, no person shall "be subject for the same offense to be twice put in jeopardy of life and limb"; so also the child of God shall not face the jeopardy of damnation again since that was faced by Christ and His saving righteousness was transferred to the believer by grace through the operation of faith.

As in the previous cases, the fault noted in verse 10 is corrected in the succeeding verses, here the first two verses of chapter two. Here is stated what should be the Christian's practical and wholesome attitude to sin. Needless to say, that attitude must not be one of denial, nor need it be one of fatalism to conclude that sinning is inevitable, for it is written that "sin shall not have dominion over you" (Rom. 6:14). The Christian is not left a defenseless, helpless victim to sin's inevitability. He is shown a Christ who not only died to put away sins committed, but He lives to prevent sins committing. His death deals with our justification and His life with our sanctification. One deals with the judicial aspect and the other with the practical aspect.

John now says, "My little children, these things write I unto you, that ye sin not. And if any man sin, we have an advocate with the Father, Jesus Christ the righteous: And he is the propitiation for our sins: and not for ours only, but also for the sins of the whole world" (2: 1,2).

John's approach is very suggestive. Only once does he address his readers as brethren. It is always as "children" literally meaning "my little born ones" referring to those he was instrumental in bringing to the place of the new birth. They were the children of God in both faith and fact. For them, sin need not be a necessity—"These things write I unto you that ye sin not." The possibility of sin in a believer's life is fully admitted. The necessity of sin in such a life is challenged and denied. They are enjoined to "sin not."

What is being considered here is not habitual sin but occasional sin. The Scriptures do not say that it is impossible for a Christian to commit incidental and occasional sin, for he is the child of two natures and he may live in the lower one as well as the higher. What the Scriptures do say, is that there is a difference between occasional and habitual sin. At no time is sin justified or excused or condoned or permitted. While provision is made for it, justification is not given to it.

The Christian ideal is that "ye sin not." To support

it we have both Christ's death and life. Christ died to put away sin from us and He lives to put away sin in us. His death destroyed its penalty in us and His life destroys its power over us.

All this means that for the Christian's present sin problem he has "an advocate with the Father, Jesus Christ the righteous. And he is the propitiation for our sins."

We have two facts to consider.

(1) *The presence of sin in a believer.*

It is indicated in the words "if any man sin." It is addressed to Christians and just now concerns them only. There is a difference between a creature's sin and a child's. When a Christian sins his sin is the offence of a child against a father. It is a family violation. In the case of an Old Testament Israelite it was a legal violation because it was the offence of a subject against a lawgiver. A Gentile's sin was a creation violation because it was the offence of a creature against a Creator. Now, however, both Jew and Gentile sin against love and mercy, for they are sinning in the face of Calvary and its provision for sin.

The Christian's offence is a family violation and is dealt with in the family on the basis of God's fatherhood and Christ's advocacy.

The condition of the offence and the correction of the offence are two different things. The offence of sin always creates a condition and God always provides a correction.

When a child of God sins it never destroys his relationship; he is still a child of God. He still has union though he has lost communion. If we sin it is still the same relationship, for the remedy is "with the Father." While sin affects one's state, it cannot touch one's standing. This remains unbroken and unsevered. Our union with God is eternal while our communion is conditional. Our communion may be preserved by "walking in the light" but whenever it is marred and broken there is a remedy. This remedy is in God's provision.

(2) *The provision for sin in a believer.*

It is found in these words, "We have an advocate with the Father, Jesus Christ the righteous." Here is the only place where the translated word advocate appears. Its original equivalent is paraclete and means a helper. When it is translated "comforter" as it is at least four times, it refers to the Holy Spirit whom Jesus promised as "another Comforter." This signifies the double advocacy with which God supports the believer. One advocate is in heaven in the person of the Holy Spirit.

In the law courts of New Testament times an advocate performed a distinctive function. It appears that "the relationship of advocate and client constituted a settled personal tie involving acquaintanceship and often kinship between the parties." He was not merely a hired pleader of one's cause. "He was his patron and standing counsel, the head of the order or the clan to which both belonged, bound by the claims of honor and family association, to stand

by his humble dependent and to see him through
when his legal standing was imperiled; he was his
client's natural protector and the appointed captain
of his salvation."

All of this is related to show that Christ is our advocate for we have "a merciful and faithful high
priest in things pertaining to God." He is qualified
because He is "Jesus Christ the righteous." Moreover, "We have not an high priest which cannot be
touched with the feeling of our infirmities; but was
in all points tempted like as we are, yet without sin."
By virtue of His work on the Cross we are in God's
family. Now by virtue of His work at the Throne we
are provided with both remedy and correction for
any violations in the family.

We must recognize both the finished and unfinished work of Jesus Christ. As our High Priest in sacrifice before God His work is finished. As Advocate
in sustaining us before the Father His work is unfinished. As Redeemer His work is finished. As Re-
storer His work is unfinished. As Saviour at the Cross
His work is finished. As Sustainer at the Throne His
work is unfinished. As Atoner for sin His work is finished. As Advocate from sin His work is unfinished.
As our justifier His work is finished. As our Sanctifier
His work is unfinished.

These things point to an important truth in life.
Our lives are both finished and unfinished. Our
standing before God is finished while our state in
the world is unfinished. As the result of redemption

we have been brought into an eternal relationship with God. Now, as the result of Christ's present advocacy, we are to be brought into a growth of life that will mature into the likeness of Jesus Christ. The goal is stated in these words, "Till we all come in the unity of the faith, and of the knowledge of the Son of God, unto a perfect man, unto the measure of the stature of the fulness of Christ."

Recognizing this goal and purpose we should remember the advocacy of Christ in our behalf and yield to Him in all surrender and devotion that His ministry may mature us in character and life.

One thing remains. Christ is said here to be "the propitiation for our sins: and not for ours only, but also for the sins of the whole world." In our concern for the Christian's sin problem, we must not forget the world's sin problem. Jesus Christ is the Christian's advocate and the world's redeemer.

The provision for sin is as extensive as the extent of sin. We are not left to piously contemplate the advocacy of Jesus in our behalf, but to remember that the world needs the benefits of His redemption. To tell it is our responsibility.

This message strikes at society's fundamental wrong. When appropriated it can brave deficits of character. It can balance the budget of morality. It can stem the tides of crime. It can stop the carnage of war. It can alleviate poverty and squalor. It can bring an old world to a new beginning.

# 3

## THE TRUE LIFE

### 2:3-11

IN THE previous chapter illumination was given; here it is verification. A standard of measurement is presented with which one may verify the reality and validity of his faith. Here are to be found the tests of Christian profession.

The U. S. Government maintains a Bureau of Standards in Washington where standard weights and measures are kept as a basis for all the nation's transactions. All scales and yardsticks must be tested and measured by the standards at Washington. It is not a matter of one merchant's opinion against another, but only what the standard says. So also in matters of faith and life, it is not a matter of one human opinion against another human opinion. It is a matter of a standard of authority. It is "what saith the Lord." The Bible constitutes a bureau of standards with regard to matters of faith and life.

We need never be in doubt as to what standard shall justify a person's faith for the Bible is sufficient. Our creeds may differ; our churches may be at variance; and our rules may be contradictory, but the ultimate in authority is the Word which cannot be gainsayed.

This leaves us with two choices of authority. We may either choose man's measuring standards or God's.

I. Man's Measurement.

Various tests are frequently employed to judge the reality of a person's profession.

*Sometimes it is feelings.* If we were to gauge our faith by our feelings, it would fluctuate with a barometric changeableness that would be very confusing. Nowhere in the Bible are we told to measure our faith by the way we feel. Salvation would be a very poor thing if it could be lost the moment discouragement overtook us.

*Sometimes it is Sabbath keeping.* This is practically the chief standard of legalistic sects. It is not the standard of the New Testament. It is true that commandments are reiterated in the New Testament as moral principle, but it is very devastating to this sectarian belief to notice that of all the Ten Commandments reaffirmed in the New Testament the only one omitted is the one concerning the seventh day. It cannot be found in all the New Testament, a fact which could hardly be considered an oversight.

*Sometimes it is ordinances.* No ceremony or observance can be a final test of faith for the simple reason that all of them may be perverted by selfish religious motives. A true faith will be sure to express itself in the observance of scriptural ordinances; but it is equally true that a false faith has also observed them by making them an end rather than a means to an end.

We must reject all these as unreliable standards and turn to the Bible's standard. That it has a standard of measurement it plainly declares.

II. God's Measurement.

The key to the verification of our faith is found in verse 3 where it reads: "And hereby we do know that we know him." Knowing God and knowing about God are vastly different things. The gnostics against whom John wrote, talked loud and long about their knowledge, yet it was a mere intellectual concept of God. It was *about* not *of*.

We are now presented with the yardstick of a true Christian's faith. It is one by which we may test every experience and judge every person. Like all authentic linear yard measures, this one has three feet to the yard. It has exactly three, one-foot sections of truth. Each one-foot section contains the same three words: "He that saith."

1. Keeping. Verses 3-5.

"And hereby we do know that we know him, if we keep his commandments. *He that saith,* I know him, and keepeth not his commandments, is a liar, and the truth is not in him. But whoso keepeth his word, in him verily is the love of God perfected: hereby know we that we are in him."

In the final analysis the proof of a man's faith is

not his language, but his life. It is not he "that saith
I know him" who has proved his faith, but he who
gives a practical demonstration of his faith by keeping His commandments. This is far more than the
ritualistic or legalistic keeping of certain ordinances.
It means purity and righteousness of life. It is far
more than the observance of a set of rules. It is the
recognition of righteousness as the law of life. In its
recognition there may be mistakes and failures,
nevertheless it is the habit of life to keep His commandments.

It is a mistake to interpret these commandments
as some set of legalistic regulations, even to think of
them as the Mosaic law. In the Old Testament they
were enjoined with a view of obtaining life. Here,
under grace, the keeping of commandments is an
evidence of life. As in the case of his Master the
Christian will say: "I do always those things that
please him" (John 8:29) It is not compulsory or obligatory obedience, but the spiritual response to a
new life. Knowing God will establish a harmony
with the laws of God; not as a list of arbitrary rules,
but as the expression of God's own nature, hence the
reflection of ours, since we have become "partakers
of the divine nature."

A true Christian faith will be corroborated by a
true Christian life. Jesus required the same test of
His immediate disciples. He said: "If ye continue
in my word, then are ye my disciples indeed" (John
8:31). They were not proved disciples because they

continued in His word as if discipleship were gained by doing. Instead, they would continue in His word because of their discipleship. In other words, their life would corroborate their faith. It was a test of living.

People who assume that they can continue in willful sin because God has made provision for sin are sadly wrong. Provision for sin is never the excuse for the commission of sin. Mercy is no reason for evil. Liberty is no reason for license. The Christian ideal of life is "that ye sin not."

In this first measurement of a true Christian faith the test is a positive one, not a negative one. It concludes that the proof of knowing God is not that we omit what is evil, but rather that we do what is good. Yet, it is invariably true that men and women endeavor to justify themselves by a negative test. They say, I do not lie, steal, cheat, etc. These do not constitute a true test of faith. It would be just as sensible to test life by saying I do not drink poison, cut my throat or gouge out my eyes. Faith is no more tested by negatives than life. A person can be negative without being positive, but he can never be positive without reflecting the negative. If and when he keeps God's commandments he certainly will not lie, cheat nor steal. Electrical energy in a motor is possible because of the attraction and repulsion of positive and negative currents. Leave out one and you have nothing. Put in both and you have motion. Put in positive obedience to God in life and you have negative abstinence from evil. The beginning is always in obedience. This proves life.

A good brother from the South began his sermon by saying: "Bretheren you is come to pray for rain. I'd like to ask one question—where is yo' unbrella?" Umbrellas would prove expectation and expectation would prove faith, and only faith would justify praying. Keeping proves obedience and obedience proves the reality of faith.

The test seems to be extended a bit further. It not only speaks here of keeping God's commandments, but His word as well, for it says: "Whoso keepeth his word, in him verily is the love of God perfected: hereby know we that we are in him." Keeping His commandments proves knowledge of God, but keeping His Word proves love of God. "The man who truly knows God does not make much of his knowledge; he is not in the habit of saying, like the gnostic: I have found out God. I know all mysteries and knowledge. I have fathomed the depths of deity; he shows his love to God by stedfast obedience to command, and in this obedience love has its full sway and reaches its work."

This profession would indicate a love for the Word of God, and the worship of God. There can be little congruity between a man's profession of God and his lack of reading God's Word and the absence of worship from his life. Knowledge will lead to love and love will be expressed by fidelity and devotion. Thus the person who says he knows God, and pro-

fesses to love God, but never reads His Word earns
the title of a religious liar.

### 2. Walking. Verses 6,7.

*"He that saith* he abideth in him ought himself also so
to walk, even as he walked. Brethren, I write no new
commandment unto you, but an old commandment
which ye had from the beginning. The old commandment is the word which ye have heard from the beginning."

The direction in which a person travels certainly
is some indication of the genuineness of his faith, for
it determines the company he keeps, and the destination he hopes to reach.

A person possessing a true Christian faith walks
as Jesus Christ walked. It is conceivable that we
might have such a faith, and not always exhibit it.
The test is that we must walk as He walked, for if
we are following Him we cannot be walking in the
opposite direction. One condition for discipleship
which Jesus demanded, and still demands is: "If any
man will come after me, let him deny himself, and
take up his cross, and follow me" (Matt. 16:24).
This means to walk as He walked. It means the
rhythm of His step, the companionship of His company, and the direction of His life.

A young skeptic once challenged an aged saint
with a taunting question: "Uncle, where is the road
to heaven?" The aged Christian's reply was: "Take
the first turn to the right, and go straight ahead."
The answer, while not couched in Biblical language

has the idea of Scripture in it. The first turn to the right will bring one to Christ, and with Him one goes straight ahead.

When one walks with Christ there will be both an effect, and an assurance. The effect will be that we will be pleasing to God. As Christ was well pleasing to the Father we will find His pleasure in following Christ.

The assurance will be that we will be kept by God. The security of our life will be in the certainty of His Word as well as the purity of our walk.

God's Word is not a new word. It is something which "ye have heard from the beginning." It is not a late discovery. The surest way is not the newest way. The right way is an old way. Anything purporting to be a new discovery or a new revelation is sure to be wrong.

The true Christian faith will stand a specific test: Was it taught from the beginning? This section is dealing with standards, and the standards are from the beginning. They are not opinions or discoveries. We are not discovering Christianity, we are "discipling" it.

Modern liberalists are like the ancient gnostics for liberalism is saying that in religion we stand at the peak of a long process of development, and are able now to look back and judge the past. True Christianity says that the perfect truth and the perfect life have appeared once for all in the past by which we are to judge everything else. The perfect truth is the

Bible, and the perfect life is Jesus Christ. All truth and life must be tested by these. Hence, we are not discoverers of new truth, but learners of old truth.

The difference between science and Christianity is the difference between an advancing knowledge, and a revealed knowledge. There are new discoveries in science because its exploration is purely human. While there may be new experiences in the Christian life, they are only possible because our previous experience has been limited, and they can only come now when we follow the truth as it was from the beginning. Thus the new is based upon the old. Is this not true of all life? New music is always based on the old musical scale. New sums are always based on the old figures. New inventions are always based on old materials. The substances of the earth have always been there from the creation. In Christ is a fullness of life, truth and experience, and it has been from the beginning.

### 3. Loving. Verses 8-11.

"Again, a new commandment I write unto you, which thing is true in him and in you: because the darkness is past, and the true light now shineth. *He that saith* he is in the light, and hateth his brother, is in darkness even until now. He that loveth his brother abideth in the light, and there is none occasion of stumbling in him. But he that hateth his brother is in darkness, and walketh in darkness, and knoweth not whither he goeth, because that darkness hath blinded his eyes."

Here is a new commandment. It is not new from

the standpoint of time, for love is as old as God. Its newness is in relation to faith. It is new because it is made by the criterion of faith, just as keeping His commandments and walking as He walks were such criteria. Love completes the threefold measurement of profession. We now have a completed and authentic yardstick. Its first foot-section is *keeping*. Its second foot-section is *walking*. Its third foot-section is *loving*.

Jesus advanced love as a test of life. He said: "A new commandment I give unto you, That ye love one another: as I have loved you, that ye also love one another. By this shall all men know that ye are my disciples, if ye have love one to another" (John 13:34,35). Prior to this, men judged fidelity to God by the keeping of the law. Jesus introduced a new test, and a conclusive proof. It was love. John reiterates it as a current test of life.

Love has different objects of affection. In verse 5 it is love of God while in verse 9 it is love of our brother. Both are restricted in the sense that it is not the love of any god or the love of every man. It is true in a general sense that our love is to be for all, but here it is specific. The word "brother" does not mean either our brother or our neighbor. It means affinity of character by being members of God's family through the new birth.

Love and hate are the extremes of our emotions. Darkness is the absence of light, but hatred is worse than the absence of love. In fact, it says here, that it is impossible, where one has the life of God and walks in the light, to hate one's brother.

Hatred apparently, is possible whenever we step out of the light. Just as before, this refers not to the habitual manner of one's life, but to incidental, and occasional failure. As it is possible to sin in other things, so is it possible to sin in this thing. One can fail in loving just as he can in living or believing. While this possibility is admitted we must be careful to notice that it is not the habitual order of life. It is the exception, but the rule is still the same, for "he that saith he is in the light, and hateth his brother, is in darkness even until now."

Love is not only a proof; it is also a preventive. It says in verse 10: "He that loveth his brother abideth in the light, and there is none occasion of stumbling in him." Stumbling means a scandal. Love prevents scandals. It prevents the scandals of divisions, quarrels and contentions among Christians.

"Every schism is a scandal. Every ill-tempered or cynical professor of religion; every irritable, churlish man who bears the name of Christ, blocks the path of life for those who would enter. The spiteful story or base insinuation, the hasty and unjust reproach, the look of aversion or cold indifference, the explosion of anger, the act of retaliation, the mean advantage taken of a neighbor, is another stone of stumbling thrown into the much hindered way of God's salvation" (Findlay).

In surveying these three parts of the standard of

measurement, notice that in each section the test is centralized in Jesus Christ. When it speaks of keeping commandments they are Christ's. When it speaks of walking, it is "as He walked." When it speaks of loving our brother it is a brotherhood founded on Christ.

There is an ancient legend of three architects who brought to an oriental king their models for a temple of the sun. The first was of stone, finely chiseled and richly polished, and as the king beheld it he could only admire and praise the splendid work. The second was of gold, and well did the architect descant on the burnished walls as they reflected in every angle and facet the image of the sun himself. But the third presented a temple of glass, so transparent that at first it was invisible, and it did not take long to show, as the sunlight poured unhindered through the transparent walls, that this was the true temple of the sun, reflecting not its own glory, but revealing and receiving in every part the glorious object to whose honor it was dedicated. This is the supreme object of the Church of Jesus Christ, and only insofar as we are revealing and reflecting Him who is our Head are we accomplishing the object for which the Church was founded.

# 4

# THE ABIDING LIFE

## 2:12-17

ONE of the problems we all have is finding things that last. Clothing does not last. Automobiles do not last. Even life as we know it naturally and physically, does not last. Our bodies deteriorate and we become senile and aged. However, there is offered us a life that does last. It is a life that "abideth forever."

The truth of this abiding life is set forth in relation to three things:

I. THE DIFFERENT KINDS OF CHRISTIANS. Verses 12-14.

"I write you, little children, because your sins are forgiven you for his name's sake. I write unto you, fathers, because ye have known him that is from the beginning. I write unto you, young men, because ye have overcome the wicked one. I write unto you, little children, because ye have known the Father. I have written unto you, fathers, because ye have known him that is from the beginning. I have written unto you, young men, because ye are strong, and the word of God abideth in you, and ye have overcome the wicked one."

All of these mentioned are members of the same

family. They are all children of God. As in all families, there are both ages and stages. Some differ in their ages; other differ in their stage of development. In verse 12 the apostle speaks of "children" as those who have been born into the family of God. In verse 13, however, the "children" are infants and novices in experience. In the first instance, it is the age and in the second it is the stage.

In any group of Christians one will find various stages of progress and spirituality. Some are mature, some are immature and some are in a state of suspension in between. Without making any critical distinctions in John's classification we find this true of those to whom he writes.

1. Little Children.

Childhood is the age of growing and knowing. Life is given over to the natural function of development. Its purpose is to mature. We fear to lose our children by having them grow up, but we live to regret forever an undeveloped child. We should "as newborn babes, desire the sincere milk of the word, that ye may grow thereby" (I Pet. 2:2).

2. Young Men.

Here is the picture of strength in maturity. It is the picture of conquest and adventure. It sets forth the ideal of spiritual vigor.

If the church of tomorrow is to be strong and virile its hope lies in the youths which it now nourishes. Look well to these for a man's life is settled before he becomes thirty years of age. They must be nurtured on the high and noble things of life, the source of which is the Bible.

3. Fathers.

These are fathers in the faith. They are rich in faith and ripe in grace. The faith of our fathers would not be much to sing about if there had been no evidences of maturity in their lives. However, advanced years do not necessarily mean advanced faith. Many bend with the weight of years whose Christian experience is still in the kindergarten stage. There are not many fathers in the faith, sad to say.

The secret of the young men who were overcomers lay in the fact that the Word of God was abiding in them. It made them righteous and strong. It gave them knowledge and ability. It is the great implementing force of Christian experience. None can be masters of life who do not make much of the Bible.

## II. The Wrong Kind of Love. Verses 15, 16.

"Love not the world, neither the things that are in the world. If any man love the world, the love of the Father is not in him. For all that is in the world, the lust of the flesh, and the lust of the eyes, and the pride of life, is not of the Father, but is of the world."

Christians are enjoined to not love the world, yet we are told that "God so loved the world that he gave his only begotten Son." The motives here are different. God loves the world in order to save it from its sin; men love the world for its sin. God's love is one of compassion; man's is one of indulgence. God's love is sacrificial; man's is selfish. It is the object of our life which determines its right of existence.

Two questions will aid us in gathering together the teaching of these verses.

1. What is the World?

It is here the kosmos. It is not the world as a habitable land, but the world as an arrangement of life. It is what men do in the world. It is its society, its morals and principles. It is not the world as a sphere, but as an atmosphere of life. It is the ethical conceptions of the men and women of the world. It is mankind alien and hostile to God. All of this comprises a world system, or arrangement which we are not to love.

It does not mean the world which God has made. This world with its lovely nature and changing seasons; its flowers and trees, and its lakes and seas is a thing of beauty. It possesses a cultural value which it is well for us to exploit.

Neither does it mean the world of human relations. Here are duties involving life and business. Here are responsibilities to family and community. Here are friendship and associations involving both joy and tears. This world is rich in the promises it holds for life.

The world we are not to love is the world man has made, full of sin and godlessness. It is the world lying in the power of the wicked one. It is the world which rejected Christ, and still rejects Him. It is impossible, says Scripture, to hold love for such a world, and love for God at the same time. One cannot go in opposite directions at the same time. The principles of the ungodly, and the practice of godliness cannot come out of the same experience. We cannot divide our loyalties.

We should carefully note the fact that the Bible nowhere draws a line between what is worldly and unworldly. It never distinguishes between the forbidden and the permissible. It does not make a list of taboos for the simple reason that while practices differ in different ages and places, principles remain the same. It is the principle that determines what we should do or not do. The decision is always and everywhere in Scripture a matter for the individual conscience. It is based on the inviolate principle of Christian liberty in the light of the Scriptures.

We make lists of worldly pastimes and indulgences such as card playing, dancing, smoking, etc., yet the Bible says nothing about these practices by name. It declares the principle. We are quick to classify worldly Christians by certain acts, yet the Bible does not do this. There are many people who disdainfully refrain from every one of these so-called worldly practices who are just as worldly as the people whom they condemn. Worldliness goes back of practice to principle. It is possible to be worldly without indulging in a single thing that we have classified as worldly.

The Bible tells us that worldliness originates within. It is in our love and desire. It is whatever contradicts the truth of God. It is whatever destroys fellowship with God. It is whatever dulls our spiritual senses. It is whatever takes away our appetite for the Word of God. It is whatever hinders our work for God, and mars our testimony in the world.

It is apparent from what one sees among Christians today that there is much hypocrisy on this point. In talking with a devoted Christian lady she remarked that she had been under the criticism of certain Christian women because she used make-up, and yet not one of these Christian women called upon this Christian lady during the time of a prolonged illness extending into several years. Not once did they exhibit a trace of Christian love and affection for one in need, yet they criticised her for worldliness.

What is Christianity? Is it not using make-up; not smoking; not dancing? That is not what the Bible says. A person can refrain from all these things and yet not be a Christian in the fullest sense of that word. It is not negative abstinence, but positive obedience. In obeying there will be abstaining, but one will not make a religion out of his negatives. Among other things the Bible says, "Pure religion and undefiled before God and the Father is this, To visit the fatherless and widows in their affliction and to keep himself unspotted from the world."

Christianity out of our own notions and not after Christ. There is just as much peril in being wrong in one direction as in the other. If we will take care of our inner love, we will be kept from the wrong and be directed to the right; we will not be paying tithes of mint and anise and cummin yet omit the weightier matters of the law such as judgment, mercy and faith. "These," says Scripture, "ought ye to have done, and not to leave the other undone." There is altogether too much of this thing today. The church is full of people who condemn certain worldly things, but utterly fail in the weightier and most important things of life. They strain at doctrinal gnats, and swallow ethical camels. They make a synthetic Christianity out of their taboos, but neglect the normal, spiritual Christianity of Jesus and the New Testament. They fight for opinions, but forget principles. They espouse fundamentals, but do not exhibit the fundamental which is love. When life is at its best, it is both negative and positive; it will do and not do; it will love not the world of men, but it will love men of the world; it will both love and live so that the world will have a practical exhibition of God in action.

### 2. Why Not Love It?

To begin with the Christian has a new affinity. His destiny is no longer associated with the world. His desires are no longer in that direction for he has an affinity to God.

There are good and important reasons why we should not love the world.

(1) *Because of his discipleship.*

Jesus prayed thus for His disciples: "I have given them thy word; and the world hath hated them, because they are not of the world, even as I am not of the world. I pray not that thou shouldest take them out of the world, but that thou shouldest keep them from the evil. They are not of the world, even as I am not of the world" (John 17:14-16).

Christian discipleship has a new sphere of interest, affection, desire and existence. Once it was a lower sphere; now it is a higher sphere. Once it was in the world; now it is in Christ. It is not now a question of whether a thing is essentially evil, but whether it is the ideal for the Christian. It is furthermore not a question whether it hurts us, but does its doing hurt others who watch us.

(2) *Because of his body.*

A Christian is a person whose body is now the temple of God. "What? Know ye not that your body is the temple of the Holy Ghost which is in you, which ye have of God, and ye are not your own? For ye are bought with a price; therefore glorify God in your body, and in your spirit, which are God's (I Cor. 6:19, 20).

Every child of God is a temple in miniature. The difference between the house where you live, and the one where you worship is not in the architecture or material, but in the purpose. It is set aside

for divine use. Consequently, there are some things
you do in your house that you would not do in God's
house, because of this difference of use and purpose. Formerly there were some things one did in
the body that now, as a Christian, cannot be done.
It is now the temple of God, and its use and employ-
ment is for a different purpose.

This does not mean, by any stretching of conviction, that a Christian must move out of the world.
He has worldly obligations and associations, but he
may go about these worldly things in an other-
worldly spirit.

To withdraw from the world does not mean that
the world will be withdrawn from us. There is a
story of a man who became a monk in his desire to
escape temptation. A few years later, an old friend
spied him over the wall of the monastery and
shouted, "Are you a holy man now. Has sin lost its
power?" The monk shouted back to his old friend,
"Well, so far as the world goes, it is not so bad; we
have shut out the world, but we brought our evil
hearts in with us! And besides, I find the devil can
climb even a ten-foot wall!"

The Christian ideal of behavior is to be in the
world, but not of the world.

Someone tells of a curious spider in South America that has a home under the water. It has the
power of forming a bubble about itself in which, like
a diving bell, it sinks to the bottom, remaining
there for hours, but breathing the air from above.

When it comes to the surface it is perfectly dry, not the slightest moisture having penetrated the atmosphere in which he lives.

So may the believer be in this world: so surrounded by a heavenly atmosphere that evil will not contaminate him.

If the Church of Jesus Christ were as afraid of worldliness as it is of holiness what a difference would be made.

Sitting on the bank of a narrow stream, one notices that the water in the middle of the stream is moving more rapidly than the water closer to the banks.

That this is not an optical illusion may be proved by the fact that a small stick or other light object thrown into the middle will travel downstream considerably faster than one tossed in close to the edge.

This difference in speed is due to the friction of the water at the sides of the stream, which is constantly being held back by rubbing against the banks, just as the bottom or base of a wave is retarded when it reaches the shallow water near the shore.

Therefore, when compared with the water near the sides, that in the center moves more swiftly, in spite of being slightly held back by the friction between it and the slower water on the outside.

But the friction between water and water is much less than that between water and a solid, so this does not materially alter the speed of the current in the center. It is the friction of like with unlike.

There are Christians who are retarded in their experience and growth. It is not because their experience is not real and genuine, but because they are like the water which is nearest the river bank, slowed by the friction of surface contact.

(3) *Because of the Church.*

The Jews, as the chosen people, were required to keep a strict and separate identity from the surrounding nations (cf Deut. 7:1-11). This was for the purpose of providing a good spiritual and moral prophylactic.

The need of this is not lessened in the New Testament where Christians are in view. They are brought into a "church" which is an "ecclesia" which means those who are called out. When a Christian is brought into this ecclesia he is therewith called out of the world. It is a distinction of identity and separation of life which provides a state of spiritual and moral prophylaxis. It is not for the purpose of making him queer and odd, and strange, and abnormal in his manner and behavior, but for both a preventive purpose and a means of identification. He is thereby identified as a Christian patterned and modeled after Jesus Christ.

(4) *Because of his life-pattern.*

The model of Christian living is a heavenly one. It is God's purpose that the will of God in heaven become the will of God on earth. This is to be done through the sons of God while they dwell on the earth. We must not put off into the future all the purposes of God as if nothing remained for the present. Neither should we apply everything to heaven, and leave nothing for this world. "For our conversation (manner of life) is in heaven from whence also we look for the Saviour, the Lord Jesus Christ" (Phil. 3:20). This refers to our citizenship since the word conversation originates in the Greek equivalent of politics. All of this means that the influence of heaven's life, ideals and purposes should be felt in our earthly existence.

(5) *Because of the world.*

It is stated here that "all that is in the world, the lust of the flesh, and the lust of the eyes, and the pride of life, is not of the Father, but is of the world."

The worldliness that is most apparent is the kind that is most frequently held up as being injurious. There is a world of desire which is more subtle and destructive than this world of doing. Many people live in this world of desire who hypocritically refrain from doing what are generally classified as worldly things. They even condemn healthy sports, recreations and pastimes as things to shun while at the same time are found guilty of indulging in this inner world of desire.

The things that are listed here, namely, "the lust of the flesh," "the lust of the eyes" and "the pride of life" are the three temptations with which Eve was tempted in the Garden, and Jesus in the wilderness. They represent the three basic desires of man, and they underlie all human action in which temptation is involved.

*"The lust of the flesh"* is the lowest and refers to our natural, physical appetites. It is the flesh of our physical nature under the control of the flesh of our human nature. There are legitimate natural desires, and illegitimate ones. Some tend to elevation and some to corruption. Some allow us the expression of noble things, and others lead to the expression of base things.

It is also true that the flesh may so control all our physical capacities, and desires so as to use the good for evil. However, the thought goes deeper to infer that the lust here spoken of means the desires of the corrupted, sensual nature of man. It is such desire as finds its expression through our physical capacities. Eve was tempted in this direction when she saw "that the tree was good for food." It was repeated in Christ's temptation when He was tempted to change the stones into bread. It is to use natural appetites to contradict a divine purpose. It is making the gratification of our physical appetites the end and goal of life. It is to live for physical gratification in every form.

*"The lust of the eyes"* is desire through the channel of the mind rather than the body. It is the appeal that comes through our aesthetic senses. Specifically it could be identified in one direction as the lust for

wealth, in another as the lust for dress, in another as the lust for immediate enjoyment. It is such lust as comes through the sense of sight, but which is conceived in the imagination of our mind. It is not entirely what we see, but what our thoughts desire in what we see. Thus this lust is the lust of taste rather than appetite. Eve was tempted in this direction when she saw that the tree "was pleasant to the eyes." It was a desire or delight to the eyes. It was repeated in Christ's temptation when the devil "taketh him up into an exceeding high mountain, and showeth him all the kingdoms of the world, and the glory of them." It is the temptation to live life for this world. It is the temptation to worship things such as power, and place rather than God. It is materialism which may be expressed aesthetically, culturally and socially, but its end and issue are as bad as when it is in corruption, for it displeases God.

*"The pride of life"* is the spirit of vainglory and conceit. In its high form it is conceit of knowledge and intellectual superiority. In its low form it is "an ostentation of worldly possessions or advantages, the disposition to 'show off' and to make other people look small." Among the early Greeks the kind of pride spoken of here meant "swagger" or "braggadocia." It is a reference to the boaster and the braggart. Eve was tempted in this direction when she saw the tree was "to be desired to make one wise." Satan had promised a wisdom like that of the gods and Eve saw in the tree a means of its attainment,

and therefore a power to do what God could do. It was a temptation to god-less independence by achieving human independence. This happens when people become wealthy, and wise. Their economic, and intellectual security creates an independence in which they can dispense with God. It was repeated in Christ's temptation when He was tempted to cast Himself from the pinnacle of the temple to prove that God gave His angels charge over His children. However, this would have been presumption rather than faith. It would have tempted God to act in an ungodlike manner for it would have put Christianity in the religious show business. It was an effort to get Jesus to display His indisputably divine powers in order to win the applause of people.

In our realm this temptation matures in many ways. It shows off our pride. It displays an independence of God. It is possible not only in materialistic matters, but in spiritual matters as well. It is possible in preachers who preach for applause; in singers who sing the gospel for show; in Christians, who pray, and testify for the same purpose. This is the most subtle form of worldliness, and it is possible to people who scorn and condemn the more flagrant forms of worldly practice and indulgence. To do these things is to be as guilty of worldliness as those who utterly abandon themselves to the arms of the goddesses of pleasure and revelry.

What is the remedy for this wrong kind of love: this love of the world that is passing away? One effort is monasticism. The monks retired from the world and took three vows, each directed at one of these three forms of temptation. One was the vow of chastity, aimed to conquer the "lust of the flesh." One was the vow of poverty, aimed to conquer "the lust of the eyes." The other was the vow of obedience which was aimed at "the pride of life."

The remedy prescribed here, however, for this wrong kind of love is the right kind of life.

III. THE RIGHT KIND OF LIFE. Verse 17.

"And the world passeth away, and the lust thereof: but he that doeth the will of God abideth forever."

None of the foregoing belong to God. They belong to something which is alien to God's plan for life. They belong to something which is transient. They have no continuity. They are destined to end; in fact, they are passing away right now. Their glory is constantly waning and diminishing. The world as a physical sphere will not pass away. It is the fashion or arrangement which is to disappear. Now it is Satan dominated. Soon it will be Christ dominated. All that was associated with the lusts of the flesh and eyes, and the pride of life will disappear. None will have existence in eternity.

When we live life at its best we live it for that which outlasts it. When life is sponsored by the wrong kind of love we give our thought and effort to the things that pass away, but when we do the will of God, we, and the things we have lived for, will abide forever.

The wrong kind of love leads to a perishing life. The right kind of life leads to a form of living that never ceases. It leads to an investment of strength, time and activity that pays eternal dividends.

This right kind of life finds its center and circumference in Jesus Christ. He is the expression of the will of God. Following Him we follow God's will; not as a set of abstract religious rules, but as a way to life and as a way of life.

### BUILD ON CHRIST

"Build on Christ and not upon regret
The structure of thy future. Do not grope
Among the shadow of old sins, but let
Thine own soul's light shine on the path of hope
And dissipate the darkness. Waste no tears
Upon the blotted record of past years,
But turn the leaf and smile, oh, smile, to see
The fair white pages that remain for thee."

—Author Unknown

# 5

## THE FALSE LIFE

### 2:18-27

ONE of the persistent problems as well as one of the perpetual paradoxes of Christianity has been the presence in it of the false principle and the false person. There has always been false teaching in the midst of the truth, and false Christians in the midst of true Christians. A false Christian is a misnomer and a misstatement for when a person is false he is not a Christian. It was so in the case of certain persons in the church of John's day. John the apostle had lived a long life, but from point of time the church had just begun its existence, yet in it was the paradox of the false and the true; evil and good; error and truth.

We presume to suppose that this is a modern condition only, but it has been true since the very beginning of the church. Before it was 60 years old John is saying, "Even now are there many antichrists." There was not one, nor a few, but many. Jesus had his Judas, and did not consider it strange. He said: "Have I not chosen you twelve, and one of you is a devil?" Perhaps we think we can understand the permissive will of God allowing a devil among

the Twelve before the Cross, but we are baffled by
the mystery of the prevalence of evil in the midst of
Christianity after the Cross.

We have been warned of such conditions in one
of the most prominent parables of Jesus. In the parable of the tares, and the wheat He speaks of the
false and the true growing together with similarity
of appearance that He suggests both growing "together until the harvest: and in the time of the harvest I will say to the reapers, Gather ye together
first the tares, and bind them into bundles to burn
them: but gather the wheat into my barn." The
wheat he identified as the children of the kingdom,
and the tares as the children of the wicked one.
(Matt. 13:24-30, 36-43). This is a picture of our age.
It explains the presence of evil among the good and
error among truth, even though it does not give the
reason.

It gives us, in prospect, the history of the church.
In almost every case, at least in enough to make it
significant, the New Testament writers have referred to the presence of the false principle and the
false person.

In the Corinthian church there was fornication
(I Cor. 5:1).

In the Galatian churches there were false teachers (Gal. 1:6-9).

In the Philippian church there were enemies of
Christ (Phil. 3:18, 19).

In the Colossian church there were heresies of

rationalism, ceremonialism, occultism and asceticism (Col. 2).

Paul wrote to the Thessalonian church about a great falling away and the Son of perdition (II Thess. 2:3).

He wrote to Timothy about those who would depart from the faith (I Tim. 4:1), and about those who had only a form of godliness (II Tim. 3:5) as well as about Demas the forsaker (II Tim. 4:10).

John writes of both the false principle, which appeared in the form of gnosticism, and the false person whom he calls antichrist. This name is not to be confused with that great personality who will come later, but is to be understood as applying to any who come to the place of apostasy and denial.

Three main thoughts dominate this section.

I. THE AGE. Verse 18a.

"Little children, it is the last time. . ."

What does the apostle mean by "the last time"? Does he refer to time as regarding himself or as regarding the whole scope of the gospel? If he spoke merely as a man, the former could have been true, but John was not writing personal memoirs, he was writing that which belonged to the Church. The fact that he speaks of antichrists indicated that he is not speaking merely of his time, for while antichrists have their place at that time, they are but forerunners of the Antichrist who will come at another time. Therefore, "the last time" refers without doubt to the time immediately previous to the termination of this dispensation.

Like the other apostles, John regarded the appearance of Christ in His second coming as being near, hence he speaks here in terms of "the last time" or more specifically the last hour.

It was not a mistake in time or in judgment to believe this, even though this "last time" has lengthened into almost two thousand years. It was a correct state of spiritual expectation in which he and we should live.

For the apostle, as a man, it was the last hour of his own life. He had lived long and usefully. He looked back on turbulent and triumphant years. He speaks to his children in the faith as a man who gives counsel and advice. It is one of warning and caution. He seeks their welfare and protection.

For the apostle, as a prophet, it was the first minutes of the last hour of a dispensation. Now, he was not looking back upon his own life, but forward into the prophetic future. He saw the features of that future in some of the spiritual conditions of his own time. What he was now concerned about was that his children in the faith might judge their times properly and be expectantly waiting for the advent of their Lord.

We, too, even much more than they, are children of the last hour. It is the same hour, but not the same part of the hour. For them it was the first minutes of the hour, while for us it may be the last

We should take care lest we develop a synthetic minutes, or perhaps seconds of the hour. While it is neither proper nor possible "to know the times or the seasons, which the Father hath put in his own power" it is fitting that every generation of Christians should view their times in terms of the last hour, lest they be found not watching when the Lord shall come.

II. THE CHARACTERISTIC OF THE AGE. Verses 18b, 19.

"As ye have heard that antichrist shall come, even now are there many antichrists; whereby we know that it is the last time. They went out from us, but they were not of us; for if they had been of us, they would no doubt have continued with us: but they went out, that they might be made manifest that they were not all of us."

At least one outstanding characteristic of this age of "the last time" is to be found in the presence of "many antichrists." It is the presence of the false person among the true Christians just as we observe the false principle among the truth.

These "antichrists" are not the Antichrist. The name itself is not found outside of two Epistles of John although the diabolic personality of this great religio-politico figure is found in numerous places in the New Testament.

The Antichrist is the great lawless one called "the man of sin" and the "son of perdition" in II Thessalonians and "the beast" in Revelation. He differs from these antichrists principally in the diabolical character of his personality, but also in the nature of his mission. When Antichrist comes he will be more than an enemy of Christ; he will do far more than oppose His work and deny the doctrine of the Christian faith. The Antichrist will be the opposition Christ. He will seek to destroy the work of Christ under the pretense of being the real Christ.

The appearance of this archdictator Antichrist is to be preceded by a falling away in the church. There will be found the prevalence of an antichristian spirit chiefly among church leaders. Paul in II Thessalonians 2:3, 4 gives a description of this falling away. "Let no man deceive you by any means; for that day shall not come, except there come a falling away first, and that man of sin be revealed, the son of perdition; who opposeth and exalteth himself above all that is called God, or that is worshipped; so that he as God sitteth in the temple of God, showing himself that he is God."

There is an Old Testament precedent for this falling away just prior to the last hour of that dispensation. In Malachi 2:7-9 we notice the defection and apostasy of the priests. "For the priest's lips should keep knowledge, and they should seek the law at his mouth; for he is the messenger of the Lord of hosts. But ye are departed out of the way; ye have caused many to stumble at the law; ye have corrupted the covenant of Levi, saith the Lord of hosts. Therefore, have I also made you contemptible and base before all the people, according as ye have not kept my ways, but have been partial in the law."

The antichrists of John's day and ours were forerunners of the Antichrist. These antichrists were de-
stroyers of the faith and deniers of Christ. This fact
is stated in this section in such plain language that
it is possible by it to identify any modern antichristian spirit. "Who is a liar but he that denieth that
Jesus is the Christ? He is antichrist, that denieth the
Father and the Son. Whosoever denieth the Son, the
same hath not the Father. . ." (verses 22, 23). Here
are to be found the antichristian liar and the antichristian lie. The liar is not made by the lie, for he
is of such character as to make the lie possible.
He is an unregenerate person who "hath not the
Father." This may include anyone in or out of the
church. It may even include those who are in the
pulpits of Christian churches or behind desks of
Christian schools.

The antichristian lie is the denial of the identity
of Jesus Christ. It is the denial that Jesus is the Son
of God; that He came in the flesh for "every spirit
that confesseth not that Jesus Christ is come in the
flesh is not of God; and this is the spirit of antichrist. . ." (4:3). The ancient docetic version of this
antichristian lie was that Christ was some emana-
tion from God who did not become man. The
modern liberalistic version of this antichristian lie
is that Christ is an exalted man who did not become
God. Both are a denial of the Father as well as the
Son for if Jesus Christ was not God in the form of
flesh, then both the revelation of God in the Bible

and the manifestation of Christ in history are untrue.

There is no doubt that these antichrists were so-called progressive leaders of their day. This is apparent from the fact that John dates the truth and the doctrines of the faith concerning Christ "from the beginning."

It was ill-advised progressiveness. One may progress in the truth, but never from it. Every kind of progress made in science has been within the realm of natural law. This law has been from the beginning. New laws have been discovered, but none have been added. Academic disgrace and scientific disaster have always attended ill-advised efforts to discard the truth of natural law. What is true in science is true in faith. All the efforts of modernists are ill-advised. They can only lead to disgrace and disaster. The truth is a settled thing "from the beginning." We go back to it, and then go on in it. Should we attempt to leave the truth, and assume it to be found in the new learning of the day we will end with a headache and a heartache.

John judged the antichristian liars and lies of his day by the truth which was "from the beginning." Their so-called progressiveness, and up-to-dateness was no mark of progress at all. It was instead, an evidence of human folly, and it proved and will prove to be a dangerous path to walk.

Dr. James Orr pointed out years ago, that it is a phenomenon of Christian history that it has never been possible to maintain for any extended period a position inconsistent with the foundation of truths of Scripture; either the adherents will return to a recognition of the final authority of the Bible, or lapse into atheism. Thus, there is an unbroken tradition, properly characterized as "the historic Christian faith," witnessed by a succession of preachers and evangelists reaching from Justin Martyr, Chrysostom and Augustine, to Calvin, Luther, Wesley, Spurgeon and Moody. There are, of course, widely differing characteristics in this preaching and emphasis, but always the same body of scriptural truth, and the same evangelical appeal.

This is important individually. The crucial point of any person's faith is the old question: "What think ye of Christ?" It is far more than an academic question about which to argue. It is a matter of revelation, and not education. To judge Jesus merely as a man is to follow historic error. To acknowledge Him as God is to follow historic faith. There may be numerous debates and diverse opinions, but no new word can be added, for both faith and error have said their last word.

For want of a better reason for their doubts some ministers have said that it does not matter whether Christ was virgin born or not. Let these same men take that idea to England and try to tell the English, who cherish a great loyalty for the royal family and their particular form of monarchial government that it does not matter who is the father of the present ruler. Needless to say, their argument would not get very far. Yet some hold the sovereign Son of God in less esteem than do the subjects of an earthly ruler. Such belief is both shameful and blasphemous.

The identity of those who have the spirit of antichrist is to be found not only in what they say about Christ, but in what happens to them. John observes that "they went out from us, but they were not of us: for if they had been of us, they would no doubt have continued with us; but they went out, that they might be made manifest that they were not all of us." They went out, they were not put out. They judged themselves. Error is self-revealing, self-judging and self-condemning.

The fact that some go out does not necessarily mean that all do. There are some who remain to exert their disturbing and evil influence. It is better when they go out for then their withdrawal is certain proof that they never possessed the true life nor shared in its fellowship. Their withdrawal is a certain manifestation of their antichristian nature.

It cannot be stated as a hard and fast rule that the false principle will always expose the false person by leading him to go out. Jesus' parable of the wheat and tares indicates that some will grow together until the harvest when there will be a final and complete and eternal division between the false and the true. Until that time comes, we are given certain safeguards.

III. THE SAFEGUARDS OF THE SOUL IN THIS AGE.
Verses 20-27

"But ye have an unction from the Holy One, and ye
know all things. I have not written unto you because ye
know not the truth, but because ye know it, and that no
lie is of the truth. Who is a liar but he that denieth that
Jesus is the Christ? He is antichrist, that denieth the Father and the Son. Whosoever denieth the Son, the same
hath not the Father: (but) he that acknowledgeth the
Son hath the Father also. Let that therefore abide in
you, which ye have heard from the beginning. If that
which ye have heard from the beginning shall remain
in you, ye also shall continue in the Son, and in the Father. And this is the promise that he hath promised us,
even eternal life. These things have I written unto you
concerning them that seduce you. But the anointing
which ye have received of him abideth in you, and ye
need not that any man teach you: but as the same
anointing teacheth you of all things, and is truth, and
is no lie, and even as it hath taught you, ye shall abide
in him."

Three safeguards are mentioned here.
1. The Spirit of God. Verse 20.

"But ye have an unction from the Holy One, and ye
know all things."

Truth is to be judged by the spirit of truth, the
Holy Spirit. Error is to be detected by the same
Spirit. He is our inner safeguard Who gives instant
illumination in all matters relating to truth and error.

Since the Holy Spirit indwells the Christian individually and the Church collectively, it signifies that

Christians constitute a grand jury of judgment whose verdict is final. The judge of truth is not the ecclesiastical hierarchy; it is not the theological expert; it is not the specialist in languages; it is not the priest. Opinions upon spiritual matters have been usually referred to professional judgment, a thing which we are here told is not right. The final place of arbitration is the Body of Christ which is constituted as such by the indwelling Holy Spirit. The Holy Spirit is the final source of authority, and since the Holy Spirit indwells the Christian, His indwelling presence constitutes a safeguard against antichristian persons and principles.

John calls this safeguard of the soul an "unction." It was what the Greeks understood as a "chrism." This meant an anointing oil and related to the holy anointing oil used in the Old Testament services of consecration and as such was typical of the Holy Spirit. It is here a symbolic expression of the Holy Spirit's presence, not in the clergy alone, but in the laity as well. It is not a blessing of oil to be applied externally, but a blessing of experience which comes when one becomes a Christian. It is our baptism into the Body of Christ. It is then that this "chrism" or "unction" is received. As such it is the inner ability to know the truth, hence John writes: "I have not written unto you because ye know not the truth, but because ye know it. . ."

These Christians had the "chrism." It gave them

an antiseptic power of life. It gave them a safeguard against evil and error. It afforded them safekeeping in a time of peril.

There is an unction for service which is the *gift* of the Holy Spirit, but this anointing comes from the *presence* of the Holy Spirit. There is, for instance, an unction for preaching which is the Holy Spirit's gift to a selected individual—"This unction comes to the preacher not in the study, but in the closet. It is Heaven's distillation in answer to prayer. It is the sweetest exhalation of the Holy Spirit. It impregnates, suffuses, softens, percolates, cuts and soothes. It carries the Word like dynamite, like salt, like sugar; makes the Word a soother, an arraigner, a revealer, a searcher; makes the hearer a culprit or a saint, makes him weep like a child and live like a giant; opens his heart and his purse as gently, yet as strongly as the spring opens the leaves. This unction is not the gift of genius. It is not found in the halls of learning. No eloquence can woo it. No prelatical hands can confer it. It is the gift of God—the signet set to His own messengers. It is Heaven's knighthood given to the chosen true and brave ones who have sought this anointed honour through many an hour of tearful, wrestling" (E. M. Bounds).

While the unction for service is a selective gift, the unction for knowing is a general privilege which belongs to the entire Christian body. John amplifies it a bit further on by saying "But the anointing

(chrism) which ye have received of him abideth in
you, and ye need not that any man teach you; but
as the same anointing teacheth you of all things, and
is truth, and is no lie, and even as it hath taught
you, ye shall abide in him" (verse 27).

We must not allow ourselves to be carried off into
an unwarranted attitude of self-sufficiency and self-
importance just because it says: "And ye need not
that any man teach you." It is dealing not with the
accumulation of the knowledge of the truth, but
with the detection of the truth. None of us, who
possess this "chrism" need any man to tell him what
is true or what is false, for he has the witness within.

Everyone of us needs the ministry of teaching to
aid us to "grow in grace and in the knowledge of
our Lord and Saviour." It was for this purpose that
Christ "gave some, apostles; and some, prophets;
and some, evangelists; and some, pastors and teachers (or more properly teaching-pastors)." We must
never arrogantly put ourselves beyond the need of
instruction through human instruments. The sense
of this verse does not set aside the importance of the
teachers, nor give any of us the right to withdraw
from the Christian community and say that we need
not that any man teach us. This is wrongly dividing
the word of truth and falsely applying its instruction, because its instruction applies only to the detection of the truth, and not to the increase of the
knowledge of truth.

2. The Word of God. Verse 24.

"Let that therefore abide in you, which ye have heard from the beginning. If that which ye have heard from the beginning shall remain in you, ye also shall continue in the Son, and in the Father."

This additional safeguard lies in a body of truth which dates from the beginning. This means that the Christian faith is a settled and complete body of truth. It is not an indefinite and unfinished knowledge which is to be the object of advancing learning. Hence, the safeguard of the Christian and of the Christian church lies in such truth as dates from the beginning. This beginning, of course, is the new beginning in Christ. Whoever holds this truth of the Word of God has an anchor for both present and future.

3. The Life of God. Verse 25.

"And this is the promise that he hath promised us, even eternal life."

Our keeping is not left to the uncertainty of human devotion and stedfastness. It is linked to the security of eternal life which is based upon the certainty of divine promise. Eternal life is not some goal to seek or prize to be won. It is an experience to enjoy and a foundation on which to build. It is not the attainment of the future, but the possession of the present. This life has already been brought into the world through Jesus Christ, and when faith is exercised in Him it becomes a fact of experience.

All this means that life eternal is to constitute a re-assurance to faith and not merely some stimulation of hope. Let us, therefore, build upon the verities of this faith, and the realities of this life. It is pertinent to ask whether one is anointed with the chrism of the Holy Spirit, or the baptismal rites of a church. Is the witness of God in one's heart, or is it just a name on a church roll? Is the truth of God a part of one's experience, or is it only an intellectual conception? Is one a sharer in eternal life now, or is it just a goal for religious striving? Does one know Christ, or just know about Him? Is Christ a reality of life, or a distant fact of history?

Upon these three safeguards rests the Christian's security in a world of evil and error. To remember and repeat them is to be constantly confident and at rest in their security.

# 6

## THE COMING LIFE
### 2:28-3:3

THE completeness of the Christian faith is seen
in the fact that it is both an anchor and an anticipation. It deals with both the past and the future.
Christ came, but He is also coming again. In this
anticipation of Christ lies our consummation as
Christians.

The central thought of these immediate verses
is Christ's appearing for us, and our appearing before Him. There is a glorious anticipation in the
knowledge that "He shall appear" and "we shall be
like Him for we shall see Him as He is." However,
it may be very disturbing to remember that at His
appearing for us we are to appear before Him, "For
we must all appear before the judgment seat of
Christ; that every one may receive the things done
in his body, according to that he hath done, whether
it be good or bad" (II Cor. 5:10).

At this appearing of Christ for us, we shall realize
the consummation of our sonship because "we shall
be like Him." At our appearing before Him, we shall
realize the confirmation of our service, whether it is

wood, hay or stubble or whether it is gold, silver and precious stones.

This appearing before Him does not immediately follow the believer's death. It is an event connected with the advent. It will be simultaneous and successive in the sense that while it occurs at the advent it will be a separate aspect of it.

Five things face us concerning His coming, and our relation to it.

## I. His Coming and Our Confidence. Verse 28.

"And now, little children, abide in him; that, when he shall appear, we may have confidence, and not be ashamed before him at his coming."

We face two possibilities at His coming: either confidence or shame. Our confidence will be the result of abiding; our shame contrarily so. Abiding means to live in fellowship with Him. It has the simple meaning of continuing or remaining in Christ. We do so by *abiding in His life* for "he that abideth in me and I in him, the same bringeth forth much fruit." This means production and a productive life will have no shame before Him. We do so by *abiding in His Word* for, "If ye abide in me and my words abide in you, ye shall ask what ye will, and it shall be done unto you." This means power and a life which exhibits the power of God will have no shame before Him.

The opposite of these will bring shame. If we

are fluctuating and vacillating in faith, life and service we will have cause for shame. But to abide in Him will make us steady and stedfast; it will save us from being hot and cold, on and off, from being brilliant one day and blundering the next. To abide in Him will give us that steady-going gait that will bring us to the goal.

Without this abiding, one will appear before Him some day with naught save the withered leaves of a wasted life. God forbid.

### BEYOND RECALL

"I dreamed I heard the quitting bell of time,
And all the wheels of life slowed down and stopped.
I crossed the threshold of my Father's house
With all the clinging soot and smirching grime
    Of earth forever washed away.

"I sat down in His beautiful abode
To feast upon the bounteous meal prepared;
While others of the household, who had ceased
Their labors earlier than I, came near,
Each glad to know that my workday of life
    Was done, and I was home to stay.

"And I rejoiced in their glad company,
And in the love of my dear Father, too,
But more than all beside, in fellowship
With my own Elder Brother, who for me
    At one time sacrificed His life.

"But though the rest and peace of this bright home
Were mine forever, I someway could not
Forget that during my short day of work,
    An hour had been idly spent.

"I asked my Father if I might not leave
The joys and fellowships of this glad place,
And go back to the labor of life's day,
So to relive that precious, wasted hour—
He could not grant me my request."

—Sadie Louise Miller

## II. His Coming and Our New Birth. Verse 29.

"If ye know that he is righteous, ye know that every one that doeth righteousness is born of him."

Being born again gives us a godlikeness of character and disposition. When this character and disposition is nourished by the Word it grows and matures. Its normal expression will be seen in righteous deeds. Doing righteous deeds is not a process which produces the new birth; it is the proof. It is based upon the fact that God is righteous and since we share the divine nature we will exhibit the divine likeness. We know that God is righteous, dealing fairly and justly with His creatures in the management of the world. The children possessing His life should be equally righteous.

This righteousness is not an incidental goodness, but a habitual practice of life. It is a righteousness which comes from being right, not just because of expediency or because it is the best policy or because it pays. It is a righteousness which originates with God, and not human nature. It is evident that many people exhibit deeds of morality who are not born of God. Such morality is the result of culture and comes from human kindness and it is the exception, not the rule. The characteristic of life apart from God is unrighteousness, although that unrighteousness may be sprinkled with moral deeds and may have the semblance of being right. Taken as a whole a godless world is an unrighteous world.

The inference here is that confidence "before him at his coming" is to be found in the living of a righteous life. Without this righteousness there will be shrinking shame. There is in this fact a great incentive for life, an incentive which should inspire the deeds of every day life.

III. His Coming and Our Name. Verse 1.

"Behold, what manner of love the Father hath bestowed upon us, that we should be called the sons of God: therefore the world knoweth us not, because it knew him not."

Name and birth are related. Our names are different because our births are different. Those who are born of God have the nature of God and consequently the name of a son of God. This new name links us with a new destiny which is associated with the vast changes which will take place in the world at Christ's coming.

We immediately become the object of two contrasting attitudes, by God on the one hand, and the world on the other.

*God's attitude is one of love.* We share new blessings and privileges in His family. We are the object of His unfailing affection. We are the subject of His daily thought and care. We are certain this love shall not fail nor waver.

*The world's attitude is one of depreciation.* It "knoweth us not." This does not mean that the world fails to take notice of us, but that its notice is one of depreciation. That is, the world depreciates the kind of Christianity that is intensely Christian. Oh yes, it pays tribute in generalities to Christianity, but let a person be intensely and Christlikely Christian and it fails to appreciate him! It was so with Christ, for the world "knew him not."

Although Jesus Christ was good enough to be kind to all men; wise enough to answer all questions and solve all problems; great enough to heal all diseases, and to raise the dead; righteous enough to die that all men might live, yet when He came unto His own "his own received him not." He was exchanged for a murderer, and hanged as a criminal.

The world of the first century would have been satisfied with Jesus' good manners, good deeds and good words, but for one thing: He insisted on His claims of Sonship with God, and He insisted on righteousness in all men. And now when Christians are like Him they are a disturbing element in a world that wants to live its own life. In such a world it is easy to be a religious Christian, but difficult to be a Christlike Christian.

One must choose whether the honor is greater to be a child of God, and a son of eternal destiny, or to be a person whom the world recognizes. The world measures its men by different standards, usually wealth and position. But God recognizes men by their new birth.

Ida Tarbell, biographer of eminent men was asked on her eightieth birthday to name the greatest persons she had ever met. She replied: "Those whom nobody knows anything about." This is quite true of those whom God counts great, and whom He uses. "For ye see your calling brethren, how that not many wise men after the flesh, not many mighty, not many noble are called; But God hath chosen the foolish things of the world to confound the wise; and God hath chosen the weak things of the world to confound the things which are mighty; And base things of the world, and things which are despised, hath God chosen, yea, and things which are not, to bring to nought things that are" (I Cor. 1:26-28).

"Gypsy Smith, the evangelist, and Amanda Smith, the colored soul-winner supreme, are miracles of divine grace. From the gypsy tent to a world throne is no farther than from a slave home and colored washtub to a parish world-wide. Bishops and states-men mighty preachers and the world's intelligentsia, presidents, kings and queens, sat enthralled alike at the feet of a 'darky woman' and learned the secrets of God. The Spirit of God who thrust forth a Luther from a miner's home, and Wesley from a small, insignificant English rectory, and Finney from a pile of law books, and Moody from a humble widow's cottage, likewise reached down to a slave abode, magnified the abilities of a colored girl, and sent her around the world to win her thousands."

## IV. His Coming and Our Change. Verse 2.

"Beloved, now are we the sons of God, and it doth not yet appear what we shall be: but we know that, when he shall appear, we shall be like him; for we shall see him as he is."

Great changes are destined to take place at Christ's coming, but none will be greater than the change that will occur in us. Our identity now is invisible since it is one of name and nature, but then it shall be visible and open because "we shall be like him." Now we possess sonship on the basis of His first coming, but then it will be son-likeness on the basis of His second coming.

At His first coming Jesus Christ became incarnate that He might become like us, but at His second coming we shall be glorified that we might become like Him. As a result of His first coming we received His life by faith, but at His second coming, we shall receive His likeness by sight.

The true state of the affairs which affect Christians cannot be judged today by sight, only by faith. "It doth not yet appear what we shall be." You cannot judge the coming world of peace by looking at a world at war. You cannot judge a world of righteousness by looking at this world of lawlessness. Truth seems now to be on the scaffold and wrong upon the throne, but the present is not the basis for the future.

It can be said of practically every form of life that "it doth not yet appear what we shall be," for every living thing begins its life in a protoplasmic similarity. The protoplasmic beginning of a worm, an eagle, a humming bird, and an elephant is a shapeless, structureless substance. Under the microscope and in chemical analysis they appear to be the same.

From looking at an ugly rose root can you prophesy the existence of a perfectly colored, velvet textured, perfumed rose? No, it doth not yet appear what it shall be. From looking at an acorn can you prophesy the existence of a great oak? No, it doth not yet appear what it shall be. From looking at a scrawny, fuzzy, awkward eaglet can you prophesy that one day it will soar with tireless wings upon the air, that it will defy the cyclone and scream at the clouds? No, it doth not yet appear what it shall be. From looking at a crawling, hairy, earthbound caterpillar can you prophesy that some day it will lift itself from the dust upon wings of multicolored beauty and make its home among the flowers? No, it doth not yet appear what it shall be.

No more can you prophesy what those who associate themselves with Jesus Christ will be like. "It doth not yet appear what we shall be." The heights and glory of the change will be that "we shall be like him," and being like Him we shall be like everything that is lovely, beautiful and eternal.

V. His Coming and Our Attitude. Verse 3.

"And every man that hath this hope in him purifieth himself, even as he is pure."

Whosoever gives serious thought and consideration to the Lord's coming will also make serious preparation. This preparation for what is coming is based upon what has already happened, for the cross and the crown are related. The person who hopes to be like Him as He is, must be made like Him as He was. The basis of our purity is His perfection.

The purity that is fitting in those who expect Him is not the negative purity by the absence of defilement; it is that positive purity which is marked by virtue, and those traits of character, as well as deeds, characteristic of Christ. In other words, our fitness is not only in what we do not do, but in what we do and who we are. It results from an assimilation of the character of Jesus in a threefold manner.

1. Assimilation by Anticipation.

This will be a powerful incentive for right living. The expectation of a house guest is always preceded by careful preparation.

2. Assimilation by Association.

Whosoever lives intimately with Christ will discover the power of His life upon him. It will be a daily incentive to righteousness.

3. Assimilation by Meditation.

Our contemplation of Jesus must have a very close

connection with His Word. This will bring a change into His likeness. "But we all, with open face, beholding as in a glass the glory of the Lord, are changed into the same image from glory to glory, even as by the Spirit of the Lord."

John's emphasis upon the Lord's coming deals with purity. Peter writes of the same thing, for he speaks on this wise, "Wherefore, beloved, seeing that ye look for such things, be diligent that ye may be found of him in peace, without spot, and blameless." Paul writes of the imminence and unpredictability of His return. Jude writes of the judgment that shall result. While James writes of the justice that will come.

### WHEN I HAVE GRIEF

"When I have grief that seems too hard to bear,
 When I am almost overcome with care,
 This is the hope which, shining bright and fair,
  Makes every shadow flee.

"My eyes will never, never weep again,
 My heart will never feel the ache of pain,
 And ev'ry mystery will be made plain
  When Jesus comes for me!

"O greatest comfort to this heart of mine!
 Oh, blessed promise! — covenant divine!
 It cannot fail! — the word, O Lord, is Thine:
  Glorious certainty!

"Then, to this future, let me look away
 And borrow courage for my task today,
 Content to watch and wait, to work and pray,
  Leaving the time with Thee."

                              —Robert Crumly

# 7

## THE CONQUERING LIFE

### 3:4-10

THE problem facing us in this section has to do with a very pertinent matter. It is the believer's sin problem. It is brought up at this point because of its identification with Christ's return in connection with which it is said, "every man that hath this hope in him, purifieth himself." The fact that purification is necessary indicates that pollution is possible. It is unnecessary to ask whether a Christian can sin or seek to determine how much or how little one can sin. The Christian ideal is "that ye sin not."

There are two opposite ideas with regard to sin.

*The perfectionist idea* states that the Christian neither can nor does sin. He is answered by the very fact that in this Epistle the question of sin is raised among believers. It is not dealing with non-Christians, but with Christians. It is to "little children" that John writes to give a remedy for sin. It would be without point to write to them about something that did not belong to them.

*The antinomian idea* states that the Christian may sin if he chooses. It is his belief that the obedience and sufferings of Jesus have satisfied the demands of the Law, making the believer free from all obligations to observe it. He is answered conclusively by such statements as these in this Epistle: "These things write I unto you, that ye sin not" (2:1). "Whosoever committeth sin transgresseth also the law" (3:4). "Whosoever is born of God doth not commit sin" (3:9).

Between these two extremes one of which says the believer cannot sin, and the other which says the believer can sin, stands the scriptural ideal, "that ye sin not."

Some think they see contradictions in the Epistle's statements on the matter of sin. In one instance, in 2:1 it says, "These things write I unto you that ye sin not," whereas in 3:6 it says, "Whosoever abideth in him sinneth not." How can one sin and yet sin not? In the first case it is speaking of falling into sin as an incidental and momentary act. In the second case it is speaking of sin as a continual or habitual practice. It is possible for the believer to commit an incidental act of sin, and for such a one there is the advocacy of Jesus Christ the righteous. It is not possible, however, for a truly and genuinely born-again believer to habitually practice sin. There is no contradiction here at all. It is making a distinction between incidental sin and habitual sin, between the character of the regenerate nature and the unregenerate nature.

The conquering life is a life which can meet the

challenge of sin. Certain considerations will provide us with both principle and power to meet this challenge. They will be found to reside in the Lord Jesus Christ. The general principle is that sinning is incompatible with the Christian life.

## I. To Sin Is Unlawful. Verse 4.

"Whosoever committeth sin transgresseth also the law: for sin is the transgression of the law."

This means far more than the transgression of some known law. It means that sin is lawlessness. There was sin in the world long before there was a written law to sin against. Sin, as such, goes beyond the act to the attitude.

This lawlessness goes beyond the Ten Commandments for it is contrary to the standards and spirit of the new life of the Christian. This makes it more than a legal problem. It is a life problem. It is something contrary to the very essence of the Christian life.

This makes sinning entirely incompatible with any profession of Christianity. It is as foreign to it as treason is to one's national citizenship.

## II. To Sin Is Unreasonable. Verse 5.

"And ye know that he was manifested to take away our sins: and in him is no sin."

Sin is as unreasonable in the practice of the Christian as it would have been in the person of Christ. He was a sinless character manifested for the purpose of taking away sin in order to bring us into harmony and perfection with Himself. Consequently, by His work on the cross we were saved from the penalty of sin. Subsequently, by His work at the Throne, we are being saved from the power of sin. Ultimately, by His return, we will be saved from the presence of sin.

In view of this, any practice of sin by a believer is unreasonable. There can be no reasonable excuse or occasion for sin in the face of the fact that Christ was manifested to "take away our sins."

This manifestation of Christ deals with the sin problem in its past and present phases.

1. To Take Away Our Past Sins.

"And ye know that he was manifested to take away our sins" (Verse 5). This referred to the guilt of sins committed. It constituted a tremendous moral and spiritual liability upon all of us. In Christ it was all taken away.

2. To Keep Us From Present Sinning.

"He that committeth sins is of the devil, for the devil s i n n e t h from the beginning. For this purpose the Son of God was manifested, that he might destroy the works of the devil" (Verse 8). Sin is the work of the devil. He introduced it into human nature. It is the present purpose of Christ that we should live, not according to our human nature, but according to our divine nature. For this reason His manifestation included not only His work on the cross, but also His intercession at the Throne.

## III. To Sin Is Unspiritual. Verses 6-8.

"Whosoever abideth in him sinneth not: whosoever sinneth hath not seen him, neither known him. Little children, let no man deceive you: he that doeth righteousness is righteous, even as he is righteous. He that committeth sin is of the devil; for the devil sinneth from the beginning. For this purpose the Son of God was manifested, that he might destroy the works of the devil."

This refers to the normal state of spirituality and holiness. These spiritual precincts are defined as being in Christ and abiding in Him. Thus, when we are observing these spiritual laws our lives will not be characterized by sinning for "whosoever abideth in him sinneth not." This refers to the present continuous tense of the act of sinning. A change has come and the course of life has been reversed so that a Christian's life is not characterized by the practice of sin.

So far, it is all negative. A Christian not only does not sin, but he also "doeth righteousness." His life is characterized by the absence of sin, and the presence of righteousness.

The secret of meeting the challenge of sin is in maintaining an unbroken fellowship with Christ for "whosoever abideth in him sinneth not." Here is a Christian's place in life. Here is the spiritual sphere in which he is to live.

When it says, as it does, at the end of the sixth

verse that "whosoever sinneth hath not seen him, neither known him," it is manifestly not speaking of a Christian. Nor is it telling us that when a Christian sins he ceases to be a Christian and becomes unborn and denatured. It is speaking of those who have never been Christians. It is contrasting the habit of a child of God with the habit of life of a child of the devil, for "whosoever is born of God doth not commit sin" but "He that committeth sin is of the devil."

## IV. To Sin Is Unchristian. Verses 9, 10.

"Whosoever is born of God doth not commit sin; for his seed remaineth in him: and he cannot sin, because he is born of God. In this the children of God are manifest, and the children of the devil: whosoever doeth not righteousness is not of God, neither he that loveth not his brother."

Some years ago Lewis Browne wrote an article in which he asked the question, "Why are Jews like that?" The answer was obvious, just because they are Jews. It is the same with the Chinese. It is the same with the human race. The trouble with human nature is human nature.

So also the children of God act in accordance with their nature, and the children of the devil act in accordance with theirs. It is the habit of some to sin because they are born that way. It is the habit of others not to sin because they are born-again that way.

To sin is unchristian because the pattern of the Christian life is Christ. While few of us or even none of us may so perfectly adapt himself to abiding in Christ so he may become exactly and perfectly like Him, yet it is true that it is provided in the Christian plan of life that he shall always grow toward His likeness. It is with us as the old German proverb says, "If it is provided that trees shall not grow into the sky, it is equally provided that they shall always grow toward the sky."

Late one winter we planted some gladiola bulbs and eagerly watched for their sprouting. Twice the proper time passed for their appearing, but there was no sign of life. We dug up one of the bulbs, and found, to our deep chagrin, that we had planted all of the bulbs upside down. But in spite of the ignorant mistake of the gardener, the bulbs were sprouting and the stalks instead of continuing to grow toward the other side of the earth changed their unnatural direction and started up. Why? The attraction of the sun and the nature of the bulb made them do so. It is the nature of flowers to grow toward the sun, and in this case they were following their nature.

During the same year our snapdragons bloomed profusely having stately, velvety blossoms which because of their height let the blooms bend over until some touched the ground. But the bent over flowers felt the influence of the sun, for the flower nature to grow toward the sun was stronger than the pull of gravity, and, in the course of a few days, they bent upward, pointing their colored faces toward the sky. In like manner the nature of every regenerated, born-twice Christian, is to grow toward the SON. It is to grow away from the gravity pull of the world. His new nature of grace inclines him toward God and purity and, if he will continually "abide in Him"—the sphere of the conquering life, thus recognizing the fact of His new nature—he will overcome the gravity pull of sin and his soul will strike out for the sky.

People may talk in artifically religious t e r m s about whether the secret of conquering and overcoming is by eradication or suppression. Neither one is scriptural in term or teaching, and neither will afford any practical gain in grace and character. The secret of conquest is a question of nature— "Whosoever is born of God doth not commit sin." The secret of the new nature is the presence of a new Master. It is not concerned so much with self-control as it is with Christ-control. It is not so much I, holding the reins of will power in my hands, who can drive the champing steeds of passion and disposition through the dangers of temptation, as it is the One who rides in the chariot beside me.

We take the miracle of oranges for granted, but years ago there were none of the sweet, seedless navel oranges that we know today. A navel orange tree was imported from Brazil and planted at Riverside, California, where old orange trees were topped leaving short trunks into which cuttings from the Brazilian navel were budded. The grafting was successful and soon the character of the orange tree was completely changed. From the graft down it was an old nature, but from the branches out it was a new nature. From the bud down it had an old seedling orange nature, but from the branches out it had a seedless navel nature. The orange rancher had to exercise constant care with his new tree for occasionally little shoots sprouted from the trunk under the budded branches. These had to be removed or they would bear fruit from the old nature.

Certainly this process forms the picture of the Christian. Regeneration is the implantation and the impartation of a new nature. A Christian has two natures, an old and a new one, a nature of the flesh and a nature of the spirit. He can not eradicate the old nature or he will destroy the personality, nor can he suppress the old nature for it is not subject to human control. Paul tried suppression and cried out in failure: "O wretched man that I am." We can not suppress the actions of the old nature anymore than an orchardist can suppress the shoots of the old orange tree nature that crop out. Like the orchardist, the Christian must use the pruning knife of self-judgment and cut off the shoots that come below the graft of the new nature.

This is what Paul means when he wrote to the Colossians: "Mortify therefore your members which are upon the earth; fornication, uncleanness, inordinate affection, evil concupiscence and covetousness, which is idolatry: For which thing's sake the wrath of God cometh on the children of disobedience: In the which ye also walked some time, when ye lived in them. But now ye also put off all these; anger, wrath, malice, blasphemy, filthy communication out of your mouth. Lie not one to another, seeing that ye have put off the old man with his deeds; And have put on the new man, which is renewed in knowledge after the image of him that created him: Where there is neither Greek nor Jew, circumcision nor uncircumcision, Barbarian, Scythian, bond nor free: but Christ is all, and in all" (Col. 3:5-11). God "puts in"; we "put off" and "put on."

A further illumination of this matter is found in three chapters in Romans.

*In Romans* 6 the question is: *Shall I continue in sin as a matter of choice?* This question strikes at the teaching of antinomianism which affirms that one can choose to sin because Christ has fulfilled the law. The answer is, "God forbid. How shall we, that are dead to sin, live any longer therein?" (Rom. 6:2).

*In Romans* 7 the implied question is:*Shall I submit to sin as a matter of circumstance?* This question strikes at the idea of spiritual fatalism, moral submission, and spiritual inertia—we have to sin and we cannot help it. The answer begins to take form in the last words of chapter 7: "I thank God through Jesus Christ our Lord."

The complete answer is in *Romans* 8. Paul recognizes the two natures and sees a life free from domination and condemnation by walking "not after the flesh (old nature) but after the spirit (new nature)." He concludes with words unequalled in all the Bible, verses 29-39, "For whom he did foreknow, he also did predestinate to be conformed to the image of His Son, that he might be the firstborn among many brethren. Moreover whom he did predestinate, them he also called: and whom he called, them he also justified: and whom he justified, them he also glorified. What shall we then say to these things? If God be for us, who can be against us? He that spared not his own Son, but delivered him up for us all, how shall he not with him also freely give us all things? Who shall lay anything to the charge of God's elect? It is God that justifieth. Who is he that condemneth? It is Christ that died, yea rather, that is risen again, who is even at the right hand of God, who also maketh intercession for us. Who shall separate us from the love of Christ? shall tribulation, or distress, or persecution, or famine, or nakedness, or peril, or sword? As it is written, For thy sake we are killed all the day long; we are accounted as sheep for the slaughter. Nay, in all these things we are more than conquerors through him that loved us. For I am persuaded, that neither death, nor life, nor angels, nor principalities, nor powers, nor things present, nor things to come; Nor height, nor depth, nor any other creature, shall be able to separate us from the love of God, which is in Christ Jesus our Lord."

The question of whether a Christian can or should sin reverts to the topic from which it arose. It is I John 3:3, "And every man that hath this hope in him (the hope of being changed into the likeness of Christ at His return) purifieth himself." The matter is one of personal purification because sin is personal defilement. The secret of possessing purity and lessening the danger of defilement is this "hope." The intensity of the hope measures the purity of the life. If we hold the hope intensely we shall have the purity personally.

We can not transcend this argument: Life is for the King, therefore, it must be lived with the approximation of perfection as the goal. When we live expecting the personal return of our King, the incentive of life is both transforming and purifying.

# 8
## THE LOVE LIFE
### 3:11-24

THE authority of John's message in every part of this Epistle is dated "from the beginning." This is authority by priority and is very important to keep in mind in a day when religious inventions are so multiplied. Most of these inventions are advanced upon the premise that they are new discoveries of truth. If any new religion or cult is dated from some so-called new revelation it has no authority. The truth is "from the beginning." It has neither variations nor substitutions. There may be much progress in the sphere of truth, but none away from it. The most modern experience of God is based upon this truth which is "from the beginning."

Thus far our progress has brought us in touch with two great spiritual factors, namely *life* and *light*. We advance now to a third, *love*. The life of love was manifested in the beginning to become the light of man. When this light illuminates our daily existence it will in turn be manifested by another and equally important quality, love. This provides a normal spiritual progression from life to light to love. When we have reached the latter, we have arrived at the highest point in Christian experience. "And now abideth faith, hope, love, these three; but the greatest of these is love."

What we are being told here is that love proves life. The test of the genuineness of our life is not our profession or our religious activity; nor is it church attendance, hymn singing or breast beating.

In the proof which love provides are certain definite items, such as the following:

I. LOVE PROVES OUR UNLIKENESS TO HUMAN NATURE. Verses 11, 12.

"For this is the message that ye heard from the beginning, that we should love one another. Not as Cain, who was of that wicked one, and slew his brother. And wherefore slew he him? Because his own works were evil, and his brother's righteous."

The love with which we are admonished to love one another is the reflection of a divine nature. It is the result of the believer partaking of the nature of God. Such love is not merely a friendly feeling or a sentimental affection.

The Greeks had numerous words to express love. Our word, which was identified with their Goddess of love Aphrodite, was used in speaking of her son. It denoted love of a sensual nature. This word *eros* is not once used in the New Testament. Then, they had another word denoting friendly affection, *phileo*, but this is not the word that is used here when it tells us "that we should love one another."

The word for love at this point is another word, *agapao*, which denotes a love that reaches behind human nature to God so that those who possess this love prove by its possession and expression their likeness to God and consequently their unlikeness to human nature.

This kind of love refers to a spiritual and godlike affection. By it we prove our new nature. By it we prove that our new nature is godlike and not according to the old standards of our previous life and our old nature.

This fact is illustrated in Cain, the man who was not only the first son of Adam, but also the leader of the branch of the race which followed the natural course of a fallen, sinful human nature. Cain and his posterity became city builders, industrialists, capitalists, artists, agriculturalists; they engaged in all of the industries, crafts and arts of civilization. But in spite of this development, Cain was a wanderer, a religious murderer, killing his brother in a moment of religious jealousy. The point is, that whoever possesses God's nature has also God's love and becomes not only unlike Cain, but also unlike the whole order of Cainitic civilization, to which our twentieth century civilization belongs.

The one sin mentioned concerning Cain is murder. It is the greatest of natural sins. Contrasting it is hatred, the greatest of spiritual sins. Murder is as natural to human nature as lying, thieving and immorality.

John is here addressing the disciples to their responsibility to "love one another." It would constitute the greatest proof of the change in their lives. It would prove how far they had come from the cursing, conniving and uncouth fishermen and tradesmen they were before the Lord transformed them by His grace.

If we were to measure these early disciples by what they became we must then judge them in the light of what they once were. Essential greatness is measured not by how far a man has come, but by how far he has come from where he started.

Here were men who were showing how far they had come by their love. It was proving how unlike they were to their former selves by how much they were like their Lord. It is "by this" that all men shall know "that ye are my disciples."

As the absence of sinning is the negative characteristic of the Christian life so the presence of love is the positive characteristic of the Christian life. It signifies the habit and the rule of life that we should be lovers one of another. It is in order to say here that as lesions of sin are possible so also breaches of love are possible. It is possible to step out of character where love does not control and dominate our actions. But if this is possible it is only possible as an occasional and incidental action. It is equally impossible to consistently and persistently hate for "whosoever hateth his brother is a mur-

derer: and ye know that no murderer hath eternal
life abiding in him."

II. Love Proves Our Unlikeness to the World.
Verse 13.

"Marvel not, my brethren, if the world hate you."

The believer's identity begins with his new nature. This sets him apart from the world and he
must not be surprised when the world exhibits its
hatred of him. But when a Christian exhibits hatred
we have a right to be surprised and astonished because love, not hatred, is the thing most naturally
expected of Christians. Love is not only taught by
commandment from the beginning, but it is the
characteristic quality of the new nature. It is as
natural for the Christian to love as it is for the world
to hate and it is as unnatural for him to hate as it is
for the world to love.

### TEACH ME TO LOVE

"There was a time when in my daily prayer
I asked for all the things I deemed most fair,
And necessary to my life—success,
Riches, of course, and ease, and happiness;
A host of friends, a home without alloy;
A primrose path of luxury and joy,
Social distinction, and enough of fame
To leave behind a well-remembered name.

"Ambition ruled my life. I longed to do
Great things, that all my little world might view

And whisper, 'Wonderful!' Ah, patient God,
How blind we are, until Thy shepherd's rod
Of tender, chastening gently leads me on
To better things! Today I have put on
Petition, Lord — teach me to love. Indeed
It is my greatest and my only need—

"Teach me to love, not those who first love me,
But all the world, with that rare purity
Of broad, outreaching thought which bears no trace
Of earthly taint, but holds in its embrace
Humanity, and only seems to see
The good in all, reflected, Lord from Thee.
And teach me, Father, how to love the most
Those who most stand in need of love — that host
Of people who are sick and poor and bad,
Whose tired faces show their loves are sad,
Who toil along the road with footsteps slow,
And hearts more heavy than the world can know—

"People whom others pass discreetly by,
Or fail to hear the pleading of that cry
For help, amid the tumult of the crowd;
Whose very anguish makes them cold and proud,
Resentful, stubborn, bitter in their grief—
I want to bring them comfort and relief;
To put my hand in theirs, and at their side
Walk softly on, a faithful, fearless guide.

"O Saviour, Thou the Christ—Truth, ever near,
Help me to feel these sad ones doubly dear
Because they need so much! Help me to seek
And find that which they thought was lost; to speak
Such words of cheer that as they pass along
The wilderness shall blossom into song.

"Ah, Love divine, how empty was that prayer
Of other day! That which was once so fair—
Those flimsy baubles which the world calls joys
Are nothing to me now but broken toys,
Outlived, outgrown. I thank Thee that I know
Those much-desired dreams of long ago,
Like butterflies, have had their summer's day
Of brief enchantment, and have gone. I pray
For better things. Thou knowest,
God above, my one desire now—
Teach me to love."

—Louise Knight Wheatley

## III. Love Proves Our New Likeness to Christ. Verses 14, 15.

"We know that we have passed from death unto life, because we love the brethren. He that loveth not his brother abideth in death. Whosoever hateth his brother is a murderer: and ye know that no murderer hath eternal life abiding in him."

What constitutes an infallible test of one's Christianity? How is it possible for one to know he is a Christian? Do we know it because we are fundamentalists? No. This is not the test. One may conceivably possess the principles of the faith and be busy in religious activity, but unless he possesses love he does not possess the highest proof.

It is too often true in fundamentalist circles that those who profess to know the most about the truth exhibit least this greatest of all criterion of faith, namely, Love.

We expect Christians to answer with chapter and verse, date and time, but we seldom ask them for the evidence of love. Yet it says, "We know that we have passed from death unto life, because we love the brethren." This is the proof of life. The main witness of the Spirit and the test of the Scriptures have their indispensible place, but never to the exclusion of love.

The highest spiritual attainment of the Christian life is least sought after. We seek the tongues of men and of angels, the gifts of prophecy, faith and wisdom, the crown of martyrs and the reward of service, yet none of these takes us to the heights. It is love that does this for "the greatest of these is love." In the face of this fact we find men splitting hairs over nonessentials and being divided into warring camps of theological dispute while the chiefest characteristic and the highest goal of Christian experience is neglected.

It speaks here of murder as applying to Christians. This is both strong and strange language. How is it possible for Christians to murder? Let us be sure to explain it and not cleverly explain it away.

Hatred in the realm of the spiritual world is the equivalent of murder in the physical world. The one is the wishful destruction of a soul and the other is the violent destruction of a life. When we hate a person the motive is the same as wishing him destroyed. Hatred in the heart is the same sin that becomes hatred of the hand, murder. Transfer hatred from heart to hand, and you have the act that sends men to the lethal chamber.

We must recognize that it is not beyond a Christian to have lapses in love, at which time in a backslidden moment, he may express a feeling of hatred. But in a genuine Christian such a feeling is quickly repented of. There is also a difference between the negative lack of an active love, and the positive possession of an active hate. Some Christians do not manifest a positive love and yet we cannot consider them murderers.

The special cultivation of a definite, active, expressive love will be the best evidence of true Christianity, and it will leave no room for a root of bitterness to spring up thereby causing many to be defiled.

At the height of his prominence as art critic. Ruskin took savage delight in attacking the work of persons he knew. He wrote to a friend saying that he hoped His unsparing criticism of his friend's painting would make no difference in their relationship. His friend replied: "Dear Ruskin: Next time I meet you I shall knock you down, but I hope it will make no difference in our friendship."

Christians should temper their judgment of other people and spare them that withering criticism so often expressed. They should be rebuked when they find delight in holding up their fellows to scorn and find enjoyment in knocking them down with verbal clubs under the pretense of doing it because of friendship.

IV. Love Proves Our New Likeness to God.
    Verses 16, 17.

"Hereby perceive we the love of God, because he laid down his life for us, and we ought to lay down our lives for the brethren. But whoso hath this world's good, and seeth his brother have need, and shutteth up his bowels of compassion from him, how dwelleth the love of God in him?

We have arrived at one of the Scripture's strategic and most significant places. We have come to the Bible's second John 3:16. It is no literary accident that both speak of love. The Gospel 3:16 speaks of God's love while the Epistle 3:16 speaks of man's love. In the Gospel 3:16 God's gift of His Son is the proof of His love for the world while in the Epistle 3:16 the Christian's gift of himself in love is the proof of both his love for God and man. In one case Christ, as God, laid down His life for us; and in the other case we lay down our life for the brethren. Both belong equally to Christian experience. We dare not quote the one and neglect the other. What claims we have upon the one contribute its claims upon us to exhibit the other.

The love of God is perceived by the redemption of the cross. It is perceived by Christ's death. Turning it about we can reason that since it was God's love that gave us our new life, then our new life should be a reproduction of God's love. So it follows that "we ought to lay down our lives for the brethren." This makes the connection between God's love and our love a very practical and demonstrable one. Because His love, gave, our love should give. Giving is the only evidence we possess that God loved us and it is the only evidence that we can exhibit that we love others.

How does one perceive the love of a wife or a husband? By the sweet words that flowed so freely during courtship? No! It is by what is given, by an exchange of lives and deeds. He gives himself and she gives herself and both keep on giving of each other all through life. In this, love is perceived and by it love is sustained.

LOVE'S QUESTION

"You say you love the flowers?
But do you love them so
You'll till the soil
With patient toil
That lovely flowers may grow?

"You say you love the souls of men?
But do you love them so
You'll sow the seed
And till the soil
With prayers and tears and toil,
Until within those souls of men
The Lord Christ is unveiled."

—Author Unknown

Love is not only a sacrifice; it is a satisfaction. Its blessings accrue to the giver as well as to the receiver. "It is one of the beautiful compensations in life that no man can sincerely try to help another without helping himself."

Just what does laying down our lives for the brethren mean? Is it martyrdom? Is that the kind of laid-down life that is required? Not at all. Our lives should be laid down as Christ's was, vicariously.

It was enough that Christ died and it will never become enough for us until we live for our faith. In John's day the greatest penalty for faith was death; in ours it is life. We are not tied to a stake to die, but we are placed in public scrutiny to live. It is not the self-surrender of our life which is involved so much as the self-surrender of our love in daily life and deeds. This means living rather than dying. It requires a new kind of heroism.

### HE DIED FOR HIS FAITH

"So he died for his faith. That is fine —
  More than most of us do.
But, say, can you add to that line
  That he lived for it too?

"In his death he bore witness at last
  As a martyr to truth.
Did his life do the same in the past
  From the days of his youth?

"It is easy to die. Men have died
  For a wish or a whim —
From bravado, or passion, or pride —
  Was it harder for him?

"But to live—every day to love out
    All the truth that he dreamt,
While his friends met his conduct with doubt,
    And the world with contempt;

"Was it thus that he plodded ahead,
    Never turning aside?
Then we'll talk of the life that he led—
    Never mind how he died."

—Author Unknown

Love is the proof of our faith and the evidence that we are possessors of the love of God. This is evident from the question of verse 17. "Whoso hath this world's good, and seeth his brother have need, and shutteth up his bowels of compassion from him, how dwelleth the love of God in him?" It is wonderful how quickly we look for a hole in the fence of obligation through which to escape our duties. And is it not surprising how many holes people find? It is much like what a Minneapolis lawyer said about one of the decisions of the Minnesota Supreme Court: "It was a pretty small hole for a court to creep out of, but it was large enough for a court that was looking for that kind of a hole." There is a possibility that we would like to apply "whoso hath this world's good" to rich people entirely. Notice the Word does not say, whoso hath this world's goods. It says *good*. The concordance reveals that the word for good is translated as follows: once it means "good"; five times it means "life"; five times it means "living." It is the same word used in "the pride of life" (I John 2:16), and is the same word used in

"She did cast in all her living" (Mark 12:44). It applies as much to the widow and the widow's mite as it does to the rich and rich man's gold, but it applies proportionately.

There is no exemption from the duty of giving for anyone. "Whoso hath this world's good, and shutteth up his bowels of compassion from him (hardens his heart against him), how dwelleth the love of God in him?" That is the great question. How can we prove love if we harden our hearts against benevolence? The presence of the benevolence of love in us for our brother in need is proof of our likeness to God and of the presence of God's love in us. The love that gave Christ to us becomes the love that gives us to man. Unless there is such love as this in us we become very selfish creatures and as one has remarked, a man wrapped up in himself makes a very small package.

To many people religion is a dam in which they impound all the benefits of grace for themselves, whereas God intends that we should be a channel through which those blessings may reach others.

V. Love Proves Our New Likeness to the Truth. Verses 18-24.

Love provides certain grounds of Christian assurance, but the love referred to is not merely a heart-held affection. It is a love which is expressed in practical benevolence, "My little children, let us not love in word, neither in tongue; but in deed and in truth"

(Verse 18). Love is a quality of life, not merely of the tongue (word), but also of the hand (deed) and of the heart (truth). When love receives such an expression in life it provides the grounds of assurance. Love provides—

1. The Assurance of the Truth. Verse 19.

"And hereby we know that we are of the truth, and shall assure our hearts before him."

The assurance that we are "of the truth" is not the result of the verbal battles of argument in which we may defend the truth. It comes when our love is one of deed and truth. "A true love will scarcely spring from a false faith. If faith works by love, it lives!" There may be defective knowledge and immature experience, but if love is of this kind it is the assurance of faith.

Lest someone presume to think that loving men and doing kindness brings salvation, let it be said that love brings only the assurance of salvation. The cause of salvation is grace, the means of salvation is faith, the evidence of salvation is love. "We cannot do anything to become a Christian, but afterward we do the things that become a Christian" (R. E. Neighbor).

2. The Assurance of an Uncondemning Heart. Verses 20, 21.

"For if our heart condemn us, God is greater than our heart, and knoweth all things. Beloved, if our heart condemn us not, then have we confidence toward God."

This is the assurance of an inner witness. It is something we have within ourselves. It is not a witness generated by our feelings or created by wishful thinking, but comes as a result of a life regulated by the truth and exhibiting love.

Within ourselves we know whether we have lived selfishly or not. We know whether we have exhibited love or not. If our heart does not condemn us neither does God. On the other hand, if our heart accuses us and reflects the absence of love then remember, God knows what we would like to forget, and condemnation shall be ours.

The peace of an uncondemning heart is the reward of love, but it is such peace that is worth any sacrifice and every effort.

3. The Assurance of Answers to Prayer. Verses 23, 24.

> "And whatsoever we ask, we receive of him, because we keep his commandments, and do those things that are pleasing in his sight. And this is his commandment, That we should believe on the name of his Son Jesus Christ, and love one another, as he gave us commandment. And he that keepeth his commandments dwelleth in him, and he in him. And hereby we know that he abideth in us, by the Spirit which he hath given us."

Our prayer life is governed by our world life. What we do off our knees is as important as what we say on our knees. Our living has a direct bearing on our praying. God does not promise that we shall receive whatsoever we ask, as if His favors are to be given on our demand. A very definite condition is involved. It says "Whatsoever we ask, we receive of him, because. . ." It is this "because" that governs the giving.

It is "because we keep his commandments, and do those things that are pleasing in his sight." Because we keep something we shall receive something. Because we do something we shall have something. Because we please Him He shall please us.

It is important to notice what this keeping and doing and pleasing means. It is very definitely not a religious bargain we make with God. It is not an exchange of favors. It is something both ethical and essential. It is our respect for the things that govern God's relation to us. It is twofold. The first is life and the second is love. Life comes as the result of our faith in Jesus Christ. "This is his commandment, That we should believe on the name of his Son Jesus Christ. . ." Believing on Him brings us divine life and this brings us into God's family where prayer is a family matter between a child and his father. Then love is to follow life for the commandment is that we should "love one another, as he gave us commandment."

This means that assurance in prayer is based on both faith and love. Without these two things prayer is religious rhetoric and a meaningless mumble of words. Prayer is based on faith in God and love toward one another.

These assurances which love provides are supported and sustained by an undergirding assurance that governs everything else. Lest love be thought of as some emotional affection and lest we ground our hopes in some fluctuating feeling John adds this significant word, "And he that keepeth his commandments dwelleth in him, and he in him. And hereby we know that he abideth in us, by the Spirit which he hath given us."

The Holy Spirit is the Christian's supreme assurance of salvation. It is factually and dispensationally wrong to ask whether one has received the gift of the Holy Spirit. He has been given and He has been received, if one is a Christian. There can be no work of salvation apart from Him. There can be no assurance of salvation without His residence within.

What is required of us is not an exterior religious experience through the artificial keeping of commandments. This may be a mechanical, religious performance and no such performance can be a test of faith. The rich young ruler had kept the commandments, yet Jesus said, "One thing thou lackest." The final test of personal Christianity is both an internal and an external one. It is the internal assurance of the Holy Spirit and the external evidence of love for "hereby we know that he abideth in us, by the Spirit which he hath given us" and again, "We know that we have passed from death unto life, because we love the brethren."

We must realize in all this discussion about life at its best that these external evidences such as love do not automatically spring up and exhibit themselves. It is true that they are inherently present for they are potential parts of the regenerated personality, but all graces must be nourished and cultivated. It is in grace that we are to grow.

Love is the characteristic of the new life. It is our life-potential. It is life's normal expression. It is possible to suppress it and to express the things that fall below this ideal, but when a Christian lives in the vigor of faith and in the strength of fellowship he will exhibit these qualities of the new life.

# 9

## THE DISCERNING LIFE

### 4:1-6

THERE is often great bewilderment over the many forms of religious matter which are being offered these days. Is it possible to know the difference between truth and error? The possibility is before us in this section and is summed up in this declaration, "Hereby know we the spirit of truth, and the spirit of error." It is possible to detect the difference.

Although we are intellectual creatures with reasoning faculties, truth and error are not identifiable by this process alone. Were this the case, truth would be accessible to the intellectual alone. The test of identification is a test of the Spirit. Truth is spoken of as "the spirit of truth" and error as "the spirit of error." In other words, it is a spiritual test.

The first sin of humanity put the human mind out of balance insofar as the perception of spiritual truth was concerned. Coveting to be as God, man saw the fruit of the tree of the knowledge of good and evil as something "to be desired to make one wise." In consequence of his desire he partook of this tree and became wise with a wisdom alienated from God and clouded by sin. Since then the human race has vainly sought to know God by processes of reason. It has endeavored to measure Him by yardsticks, test tubes, telescopes and microscopes. Man has found this search futile. While he knows much about the laws in electricity and natural forces, he does not know God. There is but one way for him to know God and that is the way of the Spirit. "But as it is written, Eye hath not seen, nor ear heard, neither have entered into the heart of man, the things which God hath prepared for them that love him. But God hath revealed them unto us by his Spirit: for the Spirit searcheth all things, yea, the deep things of God. . .But the natural man receiveth not the things of the Spirit of God: for they are foolishness unto him: neither can he know them, because they are spiritually discerned" (I Cor. 2:9, 10, 14).

However, there are tests by which we may know God and distinguish between truth and error.

I. BY THE INDWELLING OF A DIVINE SPIRIT. Verse 1.

"Beloved, believe not every spirit, but try the spirits whether they are of God: because many false prophets are gone out into the world."

The last verse of the previous chapter spoke of the Holy Spirit's presence in the believer's life. He is there, as Jesus indicated, to guide us into all truth and to teach us all things. As such He is called "the Spirit of truth" and is to be the source of our spiritual discernment.

We are admonished to "try the spirits whether they are of God." This was necessary in John's day because of many false prophets and it is equally necessary in our day for the world is full of all kinds of religious claims.

John is warning about a particular kind of spiritual error. It is found in ancient and modern forms.

1. That Evil Resides in Matter.

The gnostics claimed that matter or material substance such as our flesh, was evil; hence the way to overcome evil was to abuse and punish the flesh. It was to be achieved by a system of good works. This puts salvation on a materialistic basis and makes it the effect of human works.

2. That Evil Resides in Mind.

This is the idea that all evil originates in the mind. The salvation which is to be achieved is one of good thoughts. It is reasoned that since evil is of the mind, salvation is of the mind through good thoughts, likewise hell is only a mental state to be realized in this life, and judgment is a mental process resulting in the punishment of evil while we are here.

The Holy Spirit leads us to the truth of the matter. It is found in Scripture where we will see that evil is neither in matter nor in mind. It belongs to the spiritual realm, hence we are not told to flagellate the flesh or beautify our thoughts, but "try the spirits."

Back of all truth and error is not mind or matter, but spirit. Truth is truth and error is error before it reaches the mind or finds expression in the flesh. All truth originates with the Holy Spirit, hence it is written: "We wrestle not against flesh and blood, but against principalities, against powers, against the rulers of the darkness of this world, against spiritual wickedness in high places" (Eph. 6:12). Further we read: "The weapons of our warfare are not carnal, but mighty through God to the pulling down of strongholds" (II Cor. 10:4). What strongholds are meant? Certainly they are spiritual not physical. And so, since truth is truth, and error is error before it reaches our minds, we are charged to "try the spirits whether they are of God."

The chief reason for the impressive conquests of the primitive Christian church was the fact that Jesus trained His disciples for a spiritual battle. Today we have turned it into an intellectual battle and in some cases a reform battle, and an ecclesiastical battle. Until we return to the principles which realize that the propagandists of error and false teaching are emissaries of an evil, spiritual influence; until we lay our campaign of war on a spiritual front and use spiritual weapons, we are doomed to lose.

Not all forms of error are sponsored by a blatant atheism that seeks our forsaking of God. Satan desires the corruption of the truth as well as its destruction. We see multiplied movements t o d a y pressing the claims that they are restored pentecosts, that they possess revelations of angels and can produce miraculous powers similar to the apostolic church. Let us use care and discernment before we subscribe to these so-called new revelations and new wonders and tongues lest we become enmeshed in forms of fanatacism that will bring the truth into disrepute.

We can be sure that the Holy Spirit will never lead us into any form of Christian experience which will either contradict the Scriptures or cause us to engage in disgraceful emotional orgies such as is often the case today.

II. By the Confession of a Divine Lord. Verses 2, 3.

"Hereby know ye the Spirit of God: Every spirit that confesseth that Jesus Christ is come in the flesh is of God: And every spirit that confesseth not that Jesus Christ is come in the flesh is not of God: and this is that spirit of antichrist, whereof ye have heard that it should come; and even now already is it in the world."

Truth is identified by "every spirit that confesseth that Jesus Christ is come in the flesh." Error is identified by the denial of this fact of Christ's incarnation.

Gnosticism took this form of denial. There are other forms of the same error today.

We must not fail to notice that while there has always been a denial of Jesus Christ there has also been a difference in the denial. For instance, the modern denial does not deny that *Jesus* has come in the flesh. Almost every false propagandist believes in some form of a human Jesus. The denial today is that *Jesus Christ* is come in the flesh; in other words, the denial that the human Jesus is the divine Christ. Such denial is the spirit of antichrist, the spirit of error.

This, after all, is the supreme test: "What think ye of Christ?" The reason that this is the supreme test is that in order to lay hold of Christ as a living personality it requires an aid above man's nature and man's intellect. I Corinthians 12:3 says, "No man can say that Jesus is the Lord, but by the Holy Ghost." When Peter exclaimed, "Thou are the Christ, the Son of the living God." Jesus appraised that confession by these words: "Blessed art thou, Simon Barjonah: for flesh and blood hath not revealed it unto thee (it was not an intellectual attainment), but my Father which is in heaven." The true confessor which cries out, "Thou are the Christ," is not the human spirit but the divine Spirit in us.

This points to another important fact. The gateway of truth is not our intellect but our will. John 7:17: "If any man will do his will, he shall know of the doctrine, whether it be of God, or whether I speak of myself." The problem is not a lack of information, or revelation but a lack of disposition. Unbelieving men need disposition rather than information in order to believe. We pray for light when what we need to pray for is sight. When the blind man came to Jesus and cried for mercy, He gave plenty of sight. There was light everywhere, but they lacked the sight to see it. Today men need the divine quickening in order that they might see, and, if they will but obey, they will see.

Why is belief in the incarnation so important? It is the heart of Christianity. Had there been no incarnation, Christ would have been an apotheosis, a man moving toward God. Christianity would have been only another approach toward God. Christ would have been only a godlike man. But there was an incarnation, *God moved toward man.* Because of that Christianity is in reality God's approach to man. Christ is in fact a manlike god. The incarnation is what makes Christianity distinctly unlike any other system. A belief not founded on the incarnation is antichristian.

III. BY THE PRESENCE OF A DIVINE LIFE. Verse 4.

"Ye are of God, little children, and have overcome them: because greater is he that is in you, than he that is in the world."

In the incarnation Jesus Christ partook of our

life. In regeneration we partake of His life. Because of this participation in the nature of God we receive from Him those elements of life and truth with which it is possible to overcome both error and evil. Because of His life within us we will have light for the problems that face us. In this sense a Christian is self-contained. He has implanted within him all that life will require of him. There are no forbidding circumstances, and no threatening perils too great for him, for "greater is he that is in you than he that is in the world."

Regeneration gives us an affinity to the truth. We can remember watching great electric cranes unloading scrap metal at a large mill. Metal came to the mill in carloads, and was unloaded by means of great magnets which would be plunged into the cars, and then lifted up with large quantities of metal clinging to them and then swing over the scrap piles where the electricity was cut off leaving the metal to fall away. These magnets attracted only that which was like them. Whatever clung to them had to have an affinity to them. The same is true in the spiritual world. We will be attracted to, and we will attract that which we are like. We will have an affinity to the truth.

It may be properly expressed as a spiritual sense. Contact with error will be repulsive and contact with the truth will be responsive. It will be both spiritually instinctive and intuitive.

IV. BY THE AUTHORITY OF A DIVINE WORD. Verses
     5, 6.

"They are of the world: therefore speak they of the
world, and the world heareth them. We are of God: he
that knoweth God heareth us; he that is not of God
heareth us not. Hereby know we the spirit of truth, and
the spirit of error."

There is contrast here between what the world
says and what the Word of God says. Those who
belong to the world will identify themselves by following popular opinion. Those who belong to God
will identify themselves by subscribing to the authority of the Scriptures. Any person who knows God
will hear the Word of God. This is a sure test for by
this, "know we the spirit of truth and the spirit of
error."

There is no doubt that the world gets a larger
hearing than the Bible, but authority is not to be
judged by popularity. A judge's opinion is not always a popular one. The Bible must not be judged
by how many obey it. In John's day there were false
prophets who gained a considerable hearing, a hearing which many times was greater than that received by the apostles. This was largely true because
they accommodated their message to the palate of
the age. Truth is not to be judged by the numbers
who hear it. Its merit rests in its authority and on this
basis the authority of God's Word is supreme and
when we hold it as such it becomes the means by

which we "know the spirit of truth and the spirit of error."

It is a characteristic common to every modern cult and spurious religious system that they do not recognize the Scriptures as the final, complete and separate authority of their faith. They rely on extra revelations, or they depend, as the ancient gnostics, on a superior gnosis. It is the Bible *and* Joseph Smith, or the Bible *and* Mary Baker Eddy, or the Bible *and* Annie Besant, or the Bible *and* Judge Rutherford, or the Bible *and* Mrs. White or the Bible *and* Papal edicts.

"This completes the tests by which we are able to know the truth from the error. Four provisions are made: a divine spirit, a divine lord, a divine life, and a divine word. Using these we need not resort to the fruitless means of polemics and bigotry to maintain the faith. We do not need to denounce bigotry with equal bigotry and match shibboleth against shibboleth, until Christ has been pitifully divided and His seamless robe torn into shreds to serve for the ensigns of contending sects" (G. G. Findlay).

The one who employs these scripturally appointed tests makes them an infallible and invariable yardstick of truth. "Hereby know we the spirit of truth and the spirit of error."

# 10

## THE LOVE LIFE EMPHASIZED

### 4:7-21

LOVE has been rightly called the greatest thing in the world, but its greatness is only exceeded by the lack of its display in the world. For this reason it is brought to our attention a third time in this Epistle. In this case love follows the apostle's emphasis on the truth. We need a revival of the truth, but along with it, a revival of love. To hold the truth without love will give a grasp of the letter without the warmth of the spirit. There is altogether too much loveless Christianity. It is altogether too frequently that we see an offensive defense of the faith.

All that follows can be summed up in the simple sentence that leads it, " Beloved, let us love one another."

The reasons for this are many.

I. LOVE IS THE ESSENCE OF GOD. Verses 7, 8.

"Beloved, let us love one another : for love is of God; and everyone that loveth is born of God, and knoweth God. He that loveth not knoweth not God; for God is love."

**Love** began with God, but it must end with us. As Christians we became partakers of the divine nature and since love is the nature of God it must be exhibited through our new nature.

This kind of love is not the kind feelings of human affection, but the divine affection which was imparted at regeneration. Human affection is reciprocal—we love because we are loved. Divine affection is not a response to something outside. It is the response to Someone inside. It loves because its nature is the nature of love. It does not depend or need favorable stimuli for it is as responsive and irrepressible as the artesian well.

Twice it says, "God is love." This is God's character and not His characteristic. Men may be lovely, but only God is love. This is one of the most profound truths of Scripture yet it is one of the most widely abused. Men and women use it in a glib religious sort of fashion. They say since God is love they are safe because love can only manifest benevolence and mercy. The only safety such people have is in their own ignorance, and that is a precarious safety indeed.

It is true that God is love, but we should remember that the only way it is possible for us to share in that love is by the new birth. God's love is a filial fact that requires a family relationship before its benefits can be realized. There can be no practical knowledge or experience of the love of God except through the Son of God in whom that love is revealed, and the Word of God in which that love is recorded. The love of God was never fully known until Christ revealed it and the Bible recorded it. It does not come through physical nature. It is not perceived even in human nature.

This love of God is not simply an expression of God toward us; it is God's very nature and character. If then, we are to know it and enjoy it we must find the approach through the new birth and not through our thoughts.

## II. LOVE FOUND ITS HIGHEST MANIFESTATION IN CHRIST. Verses 9-11.

"In this was manifested the love of God toward us, because that God sent His only begotten Son into the world, that we might live through him. Herein is love, not that we loved God, but that he loved us, and sent his Son to be the propitiation for our sins. Beloved, if God so loved us, we ought also to love one another."

Three facts are set forth about this love manifested in Jesus Christ.

### 1. The Purpose of Love. Verse 9.

"In this was manifested the love of God toward us, because that God sent his only begotten Son into the world, that we might live through him."

God loved that we might live. Twice God brought life into the world. Once at the creation when He "formed man out of the dust of the ground, and breathed into his nostrils the breath of life; and man became a living soul." Once again at the redemption when He brought eternal life through His Son. Physical life came through God's breath and spiritual life through Christ's blood. In the creation the pattern was "God's image." In the redemption it is the "image of His Son." The inception of this life of ours is in the love of God which gives it prior importance both with God and man.

The revelation of God's love was through His "only begotten Son." This means that Jesus Christ was not an ordinary human being. It is referred to five times in the New Testament and always means Christ's eternal relationship to God the Father.

Being "the only begotten" means that He is different from the first Adam who was created and not begotten. He is also different from every subsequent descendant of Adam who is born and not begotten. He is likewise different from angelic beings who are of God's creating and not begetting. He is different from every Christian who is of the new birth and not an eternal begetting. In every respect and in all relationships there never has been and never will be another like the Lord Jesus Christ. He defies definition and description. He transcends all human categories and classifications. He is as unique in the annals of history as He is necessary to the experience of every human being, for there is no life apart from the love of God manifested in Him.

2. The Priority of Love.  Verse 10.

"Herein is love, not that we loved God, but that he loved us, and sent his Son to be the propitiation for our sins."

We are not saved because we love God, but only because He first loved us. His love originates and our love appropriates. The priority of saving love is on God's part for it is "not that we loved God, but that He loved us." Just how are we saved through God's love?

(1) *Because God sent His Son.*

Saving love is not an abstract thing wrapped up in some religious philosophy. It is not love as a principle which saves, but love in a person. God did not save us by His love, but by His Son. God did not say to the world, love me and be saved. God came down to the world in love personified. Thus salvation is not man's search for God, but rather God's search for and approach to man.

(2) *Because God's Son propitiated sin.*

We are not saved because Jesus lived a lovely life. It is because He died. We are not saved by His teachings, but because of His sufferings. It is not because Jesus preached the love of God, but because He propitiated the sins of man. Propitiate means to atone, and atonement means a covering. Atonement always meant the death of a sacrifice through shed blood which signified a poured-out life, resulting in a guilty sinner being able to stand in the presence of God without fear of condemnation.

3. The Product of Love. Verse 11.

"Beloved, if God so loved us, we ought also to love one another."

Since God loved us without our loving Him we ought and must love those who do not love us. It is human to love those who love us. It is divine to love those who do not love us. Here is a high standard of life and a new ideal of love. It is only possible through the new nature. Although born of God, the Christian still retains his old Adamic nature which is selfish and seeks its own satisfaction. It is only through the power of Christ living through the new nature that we can rise to this exalted standard and this high place.

III. LOVE IS THE CERTAIN EVIDENCE OF THE NEW BIRTH. Verses 12 -16.

"No man hath seen God at any time. If we love one another, God dwelleth in us, and his love is perfected in us. Hereby know we that we dwell in him, and he in us, because he hath given us of his Spirit. And we have seen and do testify that the Father sent the Son to be the Saviour of the world. Whosoever shall confess that Jesus is the Son of God, God dwelleth in him, and he in God. And we have known and believed the love that God hath to us. God is love; and he that dwelleth in love dwelleth in God, and God in him."

Men have asked for the proof of God. They say,

show me God and I will believe there is a God. One might as well ask to see the air before he believes there is air. No man has seen or can see God. It is true that "no man hath seen God at any time" and although it is said that Moses, Isaiah and Ezekiel saw God, what they saw was a theophany or form of God.

God chose to reveal and manifest Himself in the person of Jesus Christ. It is in Him that we may see God. On this fact is based another fact, namely, that as God is seen in Christ so also Christ is displayed through our love, for "if we love one another, God dwelleth in us, and His love is perfected in us."

While none of us have seen God it is not necessary that we should, for now God dwells in us by the new birth. This dwelling of God in us brings the perfection of love; not by our imitating God, but through God manifesting Himself in us. While none see God in the world they can see God in us. This is God's intention. When we walk in love men will see God in us. The question is, how much do men see of God in us? We are the only gospel some men read and love is God's great appeal.

Between verses 12 and 13 there are certain significant connections:

In verse 12 we are told that "God dwelleth in us" while in verse 13 it says "we dwell in him."

In verse 12 the proof that God dwells in us is that we "love one another" while in verse 13 the proof that we dwell in God is that "He hath given us of His Spirit."

In verse 12 the proof is outward while in verse 13 the proof is inward.

In verse 12 it is affection while in verse 13 it is assurance. The world will have proof that God dwells in us by the affection we display one to another. We will have that proof that we dwell in God by the assurance of God's Holy Spirit for "the Spirit itself beareth witness with our spirit, that we are the children of God."

While it is a fact that the divine nature is both invisible and inscrutable it is also a fact that once in human history God could be seen in the person of His Son. He was both sent by God and seen by the apostles. They were witnesses of His life and deeds. They bore testimony to His ministry and now they declared to the world that God was available to all men in a saviour.

Notice that Jesus Christ came as a saviour. He did not come primarily as a teacher, social worker, political reformer or personal example, but as a saviour. It is further true that the connection between human sinners and the divine Saviour is not imitation, reformation or education. It is confession, for "whosoever shall confess that Jesus is the Son of God, God dwelleth in him and he in God." This tells us that confession involves our faith in Jesus, not as a man nor a phantom god, but as God Himself. It further involves our reception of Him as our personal Saviour. We conclude from this that there are not many ways to the one goal. There is but one way—Jesus Christ. It is not by religion, but by redemption. It is not by works, but by faith.

IV. Love Brings Boldness before Judgment. Verse 17.

"Herein is our love made perfect, that we may have boldness in the day of judgment: because as he is, so are we in this world."

Here is supreme confidence in the face of the fact that every Christian must appear before the judgment. It is a confidence and boldness that rests in the perfection of life. This perfection does not come because we have been perfect in all things. If such were the expectation it would never be realized. The clue to its meaning rests in the word "herein." It is, "Herein is our love made perfect, . . .because as he is, so are we in this world." This means that His perfection becomes our perfection. Perfect love was displayed in Jesus Christ. He was perfect in His thoughts, in His words and in His deeds. And now that we are in Him God sees us through Him—"as he is so are we in this world." In other words, "if we live in love, then we do not fear the judgment of Christ, because then we are like Him, and He therefore cannot condemn us" (Myer's Critical Commentary).

This judgment, we take it, is not necessarily the Judgment Seat of Christ for at that place there will be many things to adjust in the life and relation of

all believers. It is rather that judicial judgment at
the Great White Throne in respect to which I stand
in the absolute perfection of Jesus Christ my Lord
and Saviour. While the believer will not be judged
at the Great White Throne it will be because of
this very perfection which he has in Jesus Christ.

We sat in a courtroom one day. It was filled with
spectators, attorneys, officers, and jury. The prisoner
entered shackled to an officer. When the courtroom
was ready the Judge's door opened and he entered.
It was a solemn scene, but no fear was felt in our
heart. We had the boldness to look straight at the
Judge and at every one there. There was no fear of
the officers with their badges and their guns. Why?
Because our name was not on the docket of cases;
we were not in the prisoner's place; there was
nothing against us. As far as the law was concerned
we were perfect. We were one of the people, one
of those against whom the offense of the prisoner
was committed. We were on the side of justice that
day. And when the great Judgment Day comes,
we will be there, not to be judged before the Great
White Throne, but to stand as a spectator. There
will be nothing against us on that day and our name
will not be called; it will not be written on the
prisoner's list, but in the Lamb's Book of Life. The
reason we shall have boldness in that day will not
rest in our excellence or perfection, but because of
Jesus Christ, who took the sin and stigma that was
upon us and nailed it to His cross. From that day to

the Judgment Day we are in this world "as he is." Because of that God will see us in Christ without sin and without condemnation. No more can we be judged than Christ can. He has been judged on the cross and so have we. Our judgment day is past. It is over and we walk through this world as Christ, not looking for judgment, but for glory. He died "as we" and we now live "as He."

V. LOVE BANISHES FEAR. Verse 18.

"There is no fear in love; but perfect love casteth out fear: because fear hath torment. He that feareth is not made perfect in love."

This fear is undoubtedly connected with the thought of judgment. Where there is perfect love there is perfect trust and consequently no fear. Since the perfection of love rests in the perfect Christ the believer can possess a perfect peace. There is a total absence of terror and apprehension as one views the future. This would not be true if the judgment depended upon how perfectly we loved and lived. Then we would all have cause to live in fear of that day. When we live in His love we are secure in that love. Then are we as He is.

Wherever love exists fear vanishes. One may have fears, but they never originate in love. A wife never fears her husband when there is love. Her husband exists to banish fear. His providing love keeps her from the fear of want. His protecting love keeps her from the fear of harm. His sheltering love keeps her from the fear of homelessness. His expressive love keeps her from the fear of lonesomeness. When such perfect love exists between God and man the same results maintain. God's saving love keeps us from the fear of being lost. God's sustaining love keeps us from the fear of failure. God's love in all respects is our guarantee of peace.

VI. LOVE VERIFIES LOVE. Verses 19, 20.

> "We love him, because he first loved us. If a man say, I love God, and hateth his brother, he is a liar: for he that loveth not his brother whom he hath seen, how can he love God whom he hath not seen?"

Our love for man verifies our love for God. If we love the brother we see, it is evidence that we love the God who is unseen. It is just as true in reverse, for if we do not love the one we see, how can we love one unseen. It is easy to talk in lofty terms about God, but this is not nearly so convincing to the world as the lowly deeds of love.

Love and hatred are incompatible. To say we love God while we hate a brother is to tell a spiritual lie. How can one profess to love the Head of the body while hating one of its members? There may be the case of one who fails to exercise a positive love toward his brother, but this is different from the absence of love which is hatred.

VII. LOVE FULFILLS GOD'S COMMANDMENT. Verse 21.

> "And this commandment have we from him, That he who loveth God love his brother also."

Love is an obligatory, not an optional, virtue. While love is a quality of the new nature and therefore a normal gift of the spiritual life, it is possible that without proper spiritual cultivation and nurture it may not have its widest expression. To check any thought of optional expression we are now told that the practice of love is appointed by God. This is the sum of all commandments, but the meaning goes even deeper than this to say that whatever love we show to God, He insists shall be shared with His other children. He refuses to accept a love we refuse to show toward our brethren. We wrong God when we are not right with man.

# 11
## THE OVERCOMING LIFE
### 5:1-12

THE Apostle John might well be called the apostle of the overcoming life since he mentions it more, probably, than any other New Testament writer. He speaks of it twelve times in the Revelation and six times in this Epistle. It forms a fitting climax to a logical progression of truth, for it leads, as it should, to victory. Life cannot be lived at its best unless it lives victoriously and triumphantly.

The subject matter of this section is set forth in three parts:

I. LOVE AND LIFE. Verses 1-3.

> "Whosoever believeth that Jesus is the Christ is born of God: and everyone that loveth him that begat loveth him also that is begotten of him. By this we know that we love the children of God, and keep his commandments. For this is the love of God, that we keep his commandments: and his commandments are not grievous."

It is a fitting beginning to a discussion of conquest that the apostle should speak again of love. This is the fourth time in this Epistle. It is one of the secrets of conquest.

In surveying the sixty years of the first century since the death of Jesus Christ the apostle could witness a vast scene of destruction and persecution. Jerusalem has been overrun. Nero's persecution lighted the fires of tribulation in every place. The entire might of Rome was set against the pitiful handful of Christians who set out to win the world. In spite of the hatred and the opposition which they encountered these people planted churches all over the empire. They had cast their nets wherever men were found. With tyranny and oppression everywhere they alone of all the peoples of the earth could say, "this is the victory that overcometh the world, even our faith."

This overcoming faith was more than a set of doctrines. It was an experience, and one of the major factors in that experience was love. Rome taught hate, but Christ taught love. Rome conquered by force, but Christians by love. It was a new weapon in an old world. It was the distinctive sign of Christianity by which all men could identify this new world-changing force.

Life is the result of faith for "whosoever believeth that Jesus is the Christ is born of God." This is important. Faith here means that the h u m a n Jesus was the divine Christ; that the man of flesh was the God eternal. Men had been trying to explain away the importance of the incarnation. It was their contention that Jesus Christ was only a phantom

God and not a real man. Today the emphasis is on the untruth that Jesus was only a great man born like other men, but with godlike qualities. This is neither true nor enough, for He was God in an eternal sense and man in a real sense.

Love is the evidence of life, for whoever has divine life will have divine love. This love will fulfill the laws of the new life which are found in the commandments of the Lord. It will be seen in an attitude to God's children as well as an attitude to God. When one is truly devoted to God he will also be devoted to those who belong to God.

II. FAITH AND VICTORY. Verses 4, 5.

> "For whatsoever is born of God overcometh the world: and this is the victory that overcometh the world, even our faith. Who is he that overcometh the world, but he that believeth that Jesus is the Son of God?"

The simple secret of an overcoming life is twofold. First to be born and then to believe.

Not all who are born of God are necessarily overcomers. The new birth gives us the potentials of victory, but actual overcoming depends on faith. The new birth implants within us all the necessities for an overcoming life, but faith puts these things to work. It takes birth plus faith. It takes power plus personality. This means that both God and man must work together. God does not do it all for us nor can we do it all for ourselves.

The negro's prayer was sound when he cried, "O Lord, help me to understand that you ain't gwine to let nuthin' come my way that you and me together can't handle."

It is the combination of a new birth and a new faith. We had faith that saved us, but there is also faith that overcomes. Succeeding faith must follow saving faith.

What is to be overcome is described here as the world. Three times it says, "overcometh the world." The world is a twofold foe.

1. There Is a World Outside.

John knew this world as a world of war, poverty, crime, evil and hatred. It hated both Christ and the Christian. Jesus told His disciples what to expect from the world—"In the world ye shall have tribulation: but be of good cheer: I have overcome the world." From it they would receive hostility and hatred, but this was not the end of it. Ultimately it was to be overcome and we could overcome it because Christ overcame. Whatever the evil enticements of the world might be, there was overcoming power in Christ.

2. There Is a World Inside.

In many respects this is more formidable. It refers to our flesh and disposition. It refers to the old nature. In miniature it is a replica of the world outside. The world outside has its response from the world inside. Jesus said that it was not what comes

from without that defiles us, but what is from within.
This inside world is the battleground of life. If we
win inside we will win outside.

In fighting any temptation the place to meet it
first is inside. A habit is best conquered from within.
A habit is simply response to a desire. Conquer this
desire and you master the habit. Defeat the world
inside and you destroy it outside. This is what Paul
meant when he said, "But God forbid that I should
glory, save in the cross of our Lord Jesus Christ, by
whom the world is crucified unto me, and I unto
the world" (Gal. 6:14).

Because of this inner world, worldliness is far
more subtle than we usually suppose. We have set
up an arbitrary set of worldly standards and judge
worldliness as consisting of worldly pleasures and
habits. Yet there are Christians who are worldly who
scorn doing these things. They sit in hypocritical
judgment upon others while they are guilty of worldliness in an even greater measure. Unloving Christians who are critical and censorious and unkind to
their brethren are guilty of it. They are equally
guilty who know no victory over the lust of the flesh,
the lust of the eye and the pride of life. Failing in the
ethics and virtues of real Christianity is a form of
worldliness that is more dangerous than any other.
There are Christians who spurn the outer worldliness who are guilty of worse forms of inner worldliness. It is far less worldly to openly indulge in a
worldly pleasure than to put on a cloak of separa-

tion to cover up truthfulness, unloveliness and deceit.

There are two worlds with but one weapon. "This is the victory that overcometh the world, even our faith." This is not only faith in our creed, but faith in our conduct as well. It is bringing all the power of Christ's victory over sin and the world on the cross to bear upon the world inside and outside. It is changing potential victory into practical victory.

III. Christ and Witnesses. Verses 6-12.

The overcoming life is always identified and related to the overcoming Christ. The certainty with which we view Him will be reflected by the manner in which we live.

If faith is the victory by which we overcome the world, we are now to understand in Whom this faith is to be placed and exactly who He is.

1. Christ and His Witnesses. Verses 6-9.

"This is he that came by water and blood, even Jesus Christ; not by water only, but by water and blood. And it is the Spirit that beareth witness, because the Spirit is truth. For there are three that bear record in heaven, the Father, the Word, and the Holy Ghost: and these three are one. And there are three that bear witness in earth, the spirit, and the water, and the blood: and these three agree in one. If we receive the witness of men, the witness of God is greater: for this is the witness of God which he hath testified of his Son."

As for Jesus Christ it says, "This is he that came by water and blood." These refer to the historic facts

of his life and death. He was inducted into His
saving ministry by the water of baptism. He accom-
plished His saving work by the blood of crucifixion.
One marks His perfect life and the other His saving
death. It required both His life and His death for
John emphasizes it in these words, "not by water
only, but by water and blood."

Redemption required both the virtuous life and
vicarious death of Christ. It required both humanity
and deity and any attempt to separate Jesus Christ
by denying the essential deity of Jesus Christ or any
effort to separate the atoning death of Christ from
His perfect life is not only untrue to the witness
of history, but the record of Scripture.

The Lord Jesus Christ has other witnesses.

(1) *In heaven.* Verse 7. These are listed as the
Father, the Word and the Holy Spirit. This is the
Trinity "and these three are one." The entire Trinity
bears witness to the divine character of the person
and work of Jesus Christ. Although this verse is considered an interpolation the point need not be emphasized for what is said is in perfect accord with
the facts of Jesus' life and character.

(2) *In earth.* Verse 8. These are listed as the
Spirit, the water and the blood. The Trinity in
heaven "are one" while this trinity on earth "agree
in one." They bear witness to the divine character
of Jesus Christ.

The *Spirit* bears witness to the divine nature of
the birth of Jesus for the angel of annunciation said

to Mary, "The Holy Ghost shall come upon thee, and the power of the Highest shall overshadow thee: therefore also that holy thing which shall be born of thee shall be called the Son of God" (Luke 1:35).

The *water* bears witness to the divine life of Jesus for at His baptism it was said, "This is my beloved Son in whom I am well pleased."

The *blood* bears witness to the divine work of atonement when Christ said, "It is finished."

In this significant manner these two trinities of heaven and earth bear witness to the divine character of Jesus and the divine work of Jesus.

All this constitutes God's witness to Christ. It is the greatest possible reason why we should believe. It is reasonable to accept human testimony when it is presented with unmistakable marks of veracity. To do so with human testimony requires that we do so with this divine testimony for "If we receive the witness of men, the witness of God is greater: for this is the witness of God which he hath testified of His Son." It is our obligation to accept it, for to do otherwise is to acknowledge our rejection of God and our denial of Jesus Christ as the Son of God.

2. The Christian and His Witness. Verses 10-12.

"He that believeth on the Son of God hath the witness in himself: he that believeth not God hath made him a liar; because he believeth not the record that God gave of his Son. And this is the record, that God hath given to us eternal life, and this life is in his Son. He that hath the Son hath life; and he that hath not the Son of God hath not life."

We can not only be sure *what* we believe but also *that* we believe for "he that believeth on the Son hath the witness in himself." Faith creates its own assurance just as it provides its own evidence. As we accepted the evidence so now we are to rest in the assurance. This assurance is not dependent upon our feelings nor is it something that comes from human pronouncements. It arises within from the Holy Spirit for "he that believeth on the Son hath the witness in himself."

Either we believe and have assurance or we disbelieve. In that case we make God a liar because we, by that very act, either discount or discredit the testimony of God concerning His Son. What is the record? "And this is the record, that God hath given to us eternal life, and this life is in his Son." It is one of the gracious provisions of God that a person may have faith in God and know why and that he may have life in God and know how. Not to know the full extent of what one has may conceivably be true, but it is hardly conceivable that a person may be in love and not know it, so also that a person have salvation and not know it.

# 12

## THE ETERNAL LIFE

### 5:13-21

IT IS very proper that in this last section of the Epistle we are given assurances of faith for a world of doubt. It is a necessary word to those who must live their lives and defend their faith in a hostile world.

The basis of assurance is faith and faith is both something to believe and something to live. We live because of it and we live by it. It is a force to be released in life.

We think of faith too much in the narrow sense of a creed. There is a higher reach of faith than that which identifies us with groups of people and statements of writing. It is faith's assurance that life is linked with God. In any dark hour this assurance will bring light. In any weak moment this assurance will bring strength; but if faith is no more than a link to a group of people or no more than an intellectual persuasion it is a very precarious thing, for the group of people may become dismembered and the statement of creed may be destroyed. Faith gives an assurance that can never be reached by destroying elements.

With this confident note of assurance John closes his Epistle, giving the assurance of faith for a world of doubt.

What a world of doubt it was! It was a pagan world saturated with mythologies, superstitions, cruelties, inequalities and a multiplicity of gods. It was inhospitable to the gospel of Christ. In all its cities the disciples met opposition, criticism, ridicule, persecution, violence and oft times death. Every branch of current though in religion, politics and philosophy was hostile to this faith.

What a world of doubt it is! Our modern world is filled with science, philosophy, education, religion and material culture but it is a world of doubt nonetheless. It has a religious respect for the generalities of Christianity but regarding the original essentials there is the same old doubt. For such a world there is the assurance of faith.

This assurance of faith has its beginning in the things we know. Seven times in these brief verses John uses the assuring words "we know." John knew and we may know. It is not necessary to be religiously vague for we may be spiritually certain. We need not qualify our faith by saying we hope or we suppose, but it may become the living, bright reality of "we know."

There is a rational faith. Such a faith may also be emotional for one cannot know without b e i n g moved deeply by his knowledge.

It is a faith which owns its own soul; which can

ratify its own convictions; which can identify its own parents and which can speak its own mind.

More than this, it is a faith which brings us into our right mind. It is not what the world calls a blind and irrational faith. Faith is the most rational and revealing thing in the world.

If the true facts were recognized and admitted it is the non-Christian who is blind. His eyes are blinded by the god of this world, and it is only re-generation by faith that can create that rationality of life in which both God and man are in their right places.

This assurance of faith for a world of doubt takes four forms:

I. THE ASSURANCE OF THE POSSESSION OF ETERNAL LIFE. Verse 13.

"These things have I written unto you that believe on the name of the Son of God; that ye may know that ye have eternal life, and that ye may believe on the name of the Son of God."

Here is the first of "these things" written to give the assurance of faith in a world of doubt. It is what we might term a knowing faith. Christianity is a religion of certainties. It provides the tests of faith by which its possessor may know what he believes and why he believes it. This assurance is neither mythical nor emotional. It is rational. It is visible and invisible. It is within and without. Within is the Holy Spirit who "bares witness with our spirit that we are the children of God." Without are the evidences of love, righteousness and all the attributes of a changed life.

This knowing faith is the normal result of a saving faith. It is first an experience and then a conviction. The conviction is based on the experience and the experience is identified by "these things" of which the apostle has written.

1. Because of a Settled Sin Question. I John 1:7-10.

If one wants to know whether a bill is paid he does not need to search his conscience for a comfortable feeling. What he needs to do is to find the receipted bill which is stamped "Paid in full." The sin bill has been paid in full and if we have fulfilled the condition of the confession of sins God has forgiven and cleansed us from those sins. It is receipted by the fact that God is "faithful and just." It is a settled and finished fact for John writes, "I write you, little children, because your sins are forgiven you for his name's sake" (2:12).

2. Because We Keep His Commandments. I John 2:4, 5.

This is a ground for assurance because it is advanced as an evidence of our new life for "whoso keepeth his word, in him verily is the love of God perfected: hereby know we that we are in him."

3. Because There Is Love. I John 3:14.

Love is the proof of life. How much love does one have to have in order to prove life? The thing in question is not quantity but quality. It is love as the general character of life. It is love as opposed to hate and service as opposed to selfishness.

4. Because of the Witness of the Holy Spirit. I John 3:24.

The Holy Spirit is the inner witness. His presence is positive assurance which cannot be changed or altered by changing life circumstances.

5. Because of the Word of God. I John 5:1.

It is written that whosoever shall believe "that Jesus is the Christ is born of God." This faith constitutes grounds of assurance because God commits Himself to save such as will commit themselves to Him.

Here are tests of faith which will yield an abundant measure of assurance, joy and happiness. They will serve to settle and establish life securely and confidently. Such assurance as this is the right of every child of God. There is a great difference between faith and the assurance of faith. Not all who have faith possess the assurance of faith. It was for this very purpose that this Epistle was written—"that ye may know that ye have eternal life, ye that believe in the name of the Son of God." It is a mistake to search one's hearts for emotional misgivings and intellectual problems, but it is greatly profitable to apply the tests which this scripture applies and to surround our life with the verities and certainties of faith.

II. THE ASSURANCE OF THE POWER OF PRAYER.
Verses 14, 15.

"And this is the confidence that we have in him, that
if we ask any thing according to his will, he heareth us:
And if we know that he hear us, whatsoever we ask, we
know that we have the petitions that we desired of
him."

This is without question one of the Bible's most
important statements on prayer. An analysis will reveal three facts about prayer.

1. Prayer Means a Conviction. "And this is the
confidence that we have in him."

This means conviction as opposed to supposition.
Prayer is not a pious probability. Prayer is an exercise of the spiritual life which is as certain in its
operation and results as the character of God. It
is our confidence "in Him." What we believe Him to
be we can know prayer to be. We can be sure and
certain of its efficacy.

This confidence means "boldness" or more literally "free speech" which enables us to express our
minds in God's presence without misgiving or fear
of embarrassment. It is complete assurance in the
divine presence.

We may not understand it but this does not lessen
our confidence which is "in Him." Thomas A. Edi-
son wrote in 1921: "We do not know the millionth
part of one percent about anything. We do not know
what water is. We do not know what light is. We do
not know what gravitation is. We do not know what

enables us to keep our feet when we stand up. We do not know what electricity is. We do not know what heat is. We do not know anything about magnetism. We have a lot of hypotheses about these things, but that is all. But we do not let our ignorance about these things deprive us of their use." Although we may not know what prayer is and how it works we do know it is the divinely appointed means of contact with God.

We cannot emphasize too much the fact that prayer is our confidence "in Him." It is so regardless of ourselves and our circumstances.

An example of this is found in Acts 7:17 where we read: "But when the time of the promise drew nigh, which God had sworn to Abraham, the people grew and multiplied in Egypt." This historical picture shows that the Jews were in a dire plight, but with it there was a promise of deliverance. The promise stated that after a certain number of years of captivity God would deliver His people. We find that history records events exactly as promised, for "When the time of the promise drew nigh, . . . the people grew and multiplied." The people did not grow and multiply gradually over the entire period of the Egyptian bondage. Were the event a human happening we might expect such a gradual increase. But it was not so. It was "When the time of the promise drew nigh" that "the people grew and multiplied." And so we see that the deliverance was not a matter of circumstances, expectation, or calculation, but it was in "the time of the promise." Remember, "the time of the promise" is God's time, not ours. Let us have this confidence in prayer—confidence in the time of promise.

2. Prayer Has a Condition. ". . . if we ask anything according to his will, he heareth us."

Prayer is based on the expression of our desires. It is required that we shall ask. We must not wait on the supposition that God knows all about us and will therefore take care of us. We must ask before He will answer. Even so, He has not promised to answer merely because we ask. There is a certain way in which to ask, "according to His will." It will be according to His will when it is according to His word. This is the condition which we must fulfill.

Also involved in this condition is the life of the person who prays, for we must live in God's will as well as pray in God's will. It would be entirely unreasonable to suppose that God would answer the prayer of a person who asked in His will while living outside His will. Faith and life, prayer and practice must coincide.

3. Prayer Brings a Conclusion. "And if we know that he hear us, whatsoever we ask, we know that we have the petitions that we desired of him."

Prayer ends by bringing us the things desired and asked for. This does not mean some time in the future. It means that as a matter of faith we have them the moment we ask. *As a matter of fact* the answer may be long in coming but *as a matter of faith* it is ours at the time of our asking.

PRAYER

"Prayer opens heavy doors all hinged with unbelief,
Prayer sheds a scented balm to assuage an aching grief;
Prayer knows no coward fear,
Notes every falling tear,
Counts every blessing here,
Knows life is brief.

"Prayer storms the hostile camps of sin and doubt and care,
Wrestling the whole night through, alive to do and dare:
Prayer meets Thee face to face,
Sensing Thy throne of grace,
Makes trial a hallowed place,
If Thou art there.

"Prayer changes grief to joy, as bud must change to flower;
Prayer yearns to bring each soul in touch with Thy great power:
Prayer looks not for reward,
Save but Thy smile, dear Lord;
Sure of Thy matchless word,
Prayer gilds each hour."

— Ruth Salway

III. The Assurance of Protection against Sin. Verses 16, 17.

"If any man see his brother sin a sin which is not unto death, he shall ask, and he shall give him life for them that sin not unto death. There is a sin unto death: I do not say that he shall pray for it. All unrighteousness is sin: and there is a sin not unto death."

Most people stop in confusion before the words "sin unto death" which is the least important item in these verses. The most important thing is the least attended to among most Christians. It is our responsibility to pray for the brother who has fallen into sin of any kind.

There are two scriptural ways to help a sinning brother. The first thing to do is pray for him as directed here. The next thing is to deal with him. That is what Galatians 6:1 tells us, "Brethren, if any man be overtaken in a fault, ye which are spiritual, restore such an one in the spirit of meekness: considering thyself, lest thou also be tempted."

Talk to God about him and talk to him about himself. These will remedy almost any situation. Our usual way is to talk about him to everyone who will listen. The greatest antidote for scandal is prayer. You can be sure that God can keep a secret. Let us quit gossiping and start praying. The knees are more potent than the tongue.

When it speaks here of the "sin unto death" it does not identify it but we may be safe in stating a few conclusions based upon Scripture. To begin with, it is not spoken of as being the sin of a Christian. Previously John spoke of a brother sinning "a sin which is not unto death." The meaning is simply this, "if a man see his brother sin in such a way that the sin which he commits does not involve absolute renunciation of Christ, and therefore does not necessarily bring condemnation with it, he shall pray for him." As the result of prayer God will give life, for sin brings with it a weakening of the spiritual life and in order that he may not continue sinning because of his depleted spiritual life, God will give him an infusion of new life.

The "sin unto death" is the sin that rejects Jesus Christ. When one does this he rejects the only means of life. There is no need to even pray for such a man. While a person is still approachable, prayer is practical but when that person comes to the place of final decision then prayer is futile.

Such a state is exceedingly rare and seldom comes to our notice. Let us not be overwhelmed by problems so rare that few people ever encounter them, while we neglect the person who is still in reach of the efficacy of prayer.

IV. THE ASSURANCE OF THE PRESENCE OF CHRIST. Verses 18-21.

This final of the four assurances of faith for a world of doubt is expressed particularly in verse 20. The apostle contents himself in the knowledge that although he is living in the midst of an evil world, he is not alone in that world. With him is the Lord Jesus Christ whose presence gives the confident assurance of the ultimate victory that will come to the Christian cause as well as the present victory that comes to the Christian disciple. It is one of the great assurances of our faith that its blessings are not all in the future. It offers all that we need for our present life.

The apostle now lists three great verities which epitomize the assurance which every Christian may enjoy in this present world. It is a threefold confession of faith beginning in each instance with the words "we know" which refer to an inner knowledge.

1. The Christian's New Ability. Verse 18.

"We know that whosoever is born of God sinneth not; but he that is begotten of God keepeth himself, and that wicked one toucheth him not."

This refers to his moral and spiritual ability to meet sin. He is still the subject of temptation and the object of satanic wiles, but since his nature has been transformed he is able to overcome these temptations.

Once it was natural to sin, now it is unnatural for "whosoever is born of God sinneth not." This means holiness of life and holiness does not mean an absolute absence of sin so much as an abhorrent sense of sin. Even though we are told "to be holy for He is holy," to achieve an absolute state of sinlessness is impossible for only God can be absolutely holy. Even so, the attitude, the direction and the abilities of the regenerated person are to "sin not."

Protection against sin lies within, "whosoever is born of God sinneth not; but he that is begotten of God keepeth himself, and that wicked one toucheth him not." The characteristic of the new nature is holiness. Holiness is possible because of the new

Master which means a new mastery over the temptation within and the tempter without.

It is said that an old negro had been a confirmed drunkard for many years without any hope of freedom from his enslaving habit. He was brought under the influence of the gospel and converted and thereafter enjoyed a complete change of life and habits. Someone, noticing the great change in him said, "So, you have gained the mastery of the devil at last!" "Oh, no," replied the new man, "I have the Master of the devil." It was the presence of the Master who gave him the mastery.

2. The Christian's New Identity. Verse 19.

"And we know that we are of God, and the whole world lieth in wickedness."

He is declared to be "of God" and distinguished from a world which lies in wickedness. He belongs to a new generation of people and a new order of life. He has new ideals and new desires because of which he lives a life which can be identified by its difference.

Being "of God" he is, according to our counting, in the minority, but that is only as the world sees it, for the fact is he belongs to the world's most powerful majority for he can say, "If God be for us, who can be against us?" This majority is invisible and the minority is visible and since the world does not live by faith it cannot appreciate the Christian's new identity.

We should remember history's lesson that God has chosen to reveal Himself through the minority. In the list of the world's religions Christianity is a minority. Narrower still is the fact that in Christendom there is a minority of those who are regenerated and not merely religious.

The hope of civilization is in this minority which Jesus called "the salt of the earth" and "the light of the world." It has been proved times out of mind to have been the last line of defense against destruction.

Corinth was the most gay and dissolute city of its times. Through it ran the commerce of Europe. It was a city of wealth, luxury, religion and philosophy but with all these, corruption. It was dedicated to the worship of Venus, the goddess of love of the Romans, later identified with Aphrodite. Their worship was lustful, not lovely. Their immorality and licentiousness gave rise and meaning to a verb commonly used to describe the worse form of immorality, namely, "Corinthianize."

In this city of Corinth was a little company of God's people. They were of the lower class for Paul says, "For ye see your calling brethren, how that not many wise men after the flesh, not many mighty, not many noble are called." Their strength lay not in their poverty and humble birth, but in their new identity, for they were "of God." They worshipped in tombs and caves. They were hated and despised. They were ridiculed and humiliated, but this minority lived on because they were "of God." In a world at its worst they lived life at its best. They surmounted Corinth's corruption and survived its destruction because they were "of God" and abided in Him.

3. The Christian's New Knowledge. Verse 20.

"And we know that the Son of God is come, and hath given us an understanding, that we may know him that is true, and we are in him that is true, even in his Son Jesus Christ. This is the true God, and eternal life."

The highest reach of human experience in relation to God is to know Him. This is realized only in Christian experience. Christian experience involves the past and the present. In the past is the incarnation when God came into history in the person of His Son, Jesus Christ. In the present is regeneration when God comes into our lives through the new birth. This causes us to "know Him that is true." This gives us a knowledge of God on a personal and intimate basis. It is not something we inherit from our ancestors, nor something we evolve from within. It is God's gift to us. It is the highest possible experience for human beings. It comes through Jesus Christ.

It proves that only in Christian experience can we have life at its best, for only in Christian experience can we know God. Knowing God is the equivalent of having eternal life. This means life as an experience and an expectation. It is life for today and forever. It is the life of God in man.

Here is something to be guarded and safeguarded. Here is something to be protected and preserved. Here is something worthy of our highest Christian devotion. Hence we are told to keep ourselves from idols. An idol is any representation of God. It is any of the conceptions of God held falsely by men. It is the human substitute for God. It is the mental conception held arbitrarily by those who do not have the true knowledge of God through Christ. Hence, it is anything that may come between a Christian and Christ. It may be a desire, an ambition, a pleasure or a friend. It is against this danger that all are solemnly warned by the apostle, "Little children, keep yourself from idols. Amen."

This is far more than an arbitrary religious restriction. It is a fundamental spiritual prophylaxis. It is a protection against spiritual disease. It is good Christian common sense. It will be the means of maintaining life at its best.

This reminds us that both faith and faithfulness are to be watchwords of the Christian life. Faith is what we believe and faithfulness is how we live. Faith is for our spiritual life and faithfulness for our world life. If we keep the faith, the faith will keep us. This is the assurance with which we are left to live life at its best.

## *Appendix*

# TESTS OF ETERNAL LIFE
## 5:13

Three times in the First Epistle of John it tells us why it was written. 1:4, "These things write we unto you, *that your JOY may be full.*" 2:1, "These things write I unto you, *that ye SIN NOT.*" 5:13, "These things have I written unto you . . . *that ye may KNOW that ye have eternal life.*"

Our field of inquiry is in the last of these three purposes, "that ye may *know* that ye have eternal life." Just what are the tests or the proofs or the evidences of the possession of eternal life? To give these proofs is one of the three purposes for the writing of this epistle and we can therefore be sure to find them present.

### I. OBEDIENCE. 2:3-6.

This first test of knowing God is obeying God. It is a life in which there is an understanding and willingness to follow God in perfect conformity. The person who has eternal life will find that one of the characteristics of that life is obedience—not forced and required but it is eager and desired. It is obedience to a person—not simply to commandments as

such. Christianity, after all, is not a set of rules. It is
fellowship with a Person—God, and when one is in
fellowship with God the easiest thing he has to do is
to obey His Word. Knowledge of any person involves understanding, sympathy, harmony and conformity and when this knowledge has come, then
people have come to the place where they are walking a parallel path. The apostle argues (vs. 6) that
there is no use saying that we know Christ and have
His life unless there is some similarity between ourself and Him, between our life and His life, between
what we do and what He says we should do.

## II. Love. 3:14-19; 4:7-12.

In many respects this is the highest test of eternal
life because love is the highest, noblest and greatest
virtue of life. "And now abideth faith, hope and love,
these three, but the greatest of these is love." When
it is human life its greatest characteristic is human
love. And when it is Christian life its greatest characteristic is Christian love. The test of loving God is
found in the fact of our loving man. The kind of love
which is here given as a test of eternal life is something more than philanthropic sympathy—it is God's
love in us and therefore a proof of God's life in us.

Several things will prove the presence of this divine love and this divine life in us.

1. There Will Be an Absence of Hatred. Verse 15.
Hatred is the equivalent of the murder of the

soul for he who hates another wishes him dead and lost. He who loves cannot hate.

2. There Will Be the Presence of Benevolence. Verse 16.

You will notice that this is the second John 3:16 of the New Testament. The first one in the Gospel of John says that "God so loved the world that he gave his only begotten Son." This second one in the Epistle of John says that we ought to so love our brother as to give ourself for him by laying down our life. God loved and gave. We are to love and give. God gave life. We are to give life.

This willingness to give life is not only found in martyrdom but equally as much in benevolence (vs. 17). "Whoso hath this world's good, and seeth his brother have need, and shutteth up his bowels of compassion from him, how dwelleth the love of God in him?"

Dying for one's faith, like the Covenanter, is one expression of love; but living for one's faith, as we may do daily by the demonstration of our love, is another form of expression.

The possession of eternal life creates a reservoir of divine love out of which flows understanding, compassion, benevolence, helpfulness and all the tender virtues of Christian affection.

III. TRUTH. 4:1-6.

Another test of life is stated in these words (vss. 2,3): "Hereby know ye the Spirit of God: Every spirit that confesseth that Jesus Christ is come in the flesh is of God: And every spirit that confesseth not that Jesus Christ is come in the flesh is not of God . . ." Here is an infallible and final test of eternal life.

How can any person have eternal life when he deliberately denies the source of eternal life? Jesus Christ in His incarnation is the source of our life and what is being denied here is not that Jesus Christ did not come but that He did not come "in the flesh" or in the reality of our human nature. And if He did not so come He could not have atoned for human sin nor brought to us the life which is eternal.

There is a "spirit of truth" and there is a "spirit of error." And we are told to "try the spirits whether they are of God." And one way we are told to try them is by our own personal attitude to Jesus Christ. How do we know Him? Who is He? What is He to us? This is an infallible test of the possession of eternal life.

IV. THE HOLY SPIRIT. 3:24; 4:13.

Dwelling in God is proved by God dwelling in His own through His Holy Spirit who makes our body His temple. The test of eternal life is not whether we can find God in a temple or a cathedral or a building but whether we can find God in ourself, our spiritual consciousness, our life, our own personal experience. Men try to associate God with buildings but God associates Himself with bodies. Acts 17:24, "God that made the world and all things therein . . . dwelleth not in temples made with hands."

In a pastor's home in Copenhagen there hung a picture titled, "The Presence." It was a study of Christ standing in the rear of a great cathedral. His person was illuminated and cast a light over the great structure. After visiting the cathedrals of Europe, I doubt the truth and fact of the picture. We found the churches of Europe famous for people—not for God. Never was reference made to the Lord's presence or power—always to their association with some famous man or some king buried in it.

The presence and possession of the Holy Spirit is the test of eternal life—not the test of a deeper life. It says here, "Hereby know we . . . because he hath given us of His Spirit." So that only by having His Spirit can we have eternal life and when we have eternal life we know it because we have His Spirit. The Holy Spirit is the proof of what kind of Christians we are. It is not whether we have all the Holy Spirit but whether the Holy Spirit has all of us, therefore "I beseech you therefore, brethren, by the mercies of God, that ye present your bodies a living sacrifice, holy, acceptable unto God, which is your reasonable service" (Rom. 12:1).

V. What We Believe. 4:15; 5:1.

This is not now the content of our faith so much as it is the object of our faith. Before, it was the content of faith concerning the incarnation of Christ.

Here, it is the object of our faith concerning the
deity of Jesus Christ. Both the content of faith and
the object of faith are tests of eternal life.

What we believe about Jesus Christ is important
and specifically His deity. This is so for two reasons:
First, because only our belief in His deity can produce eternal life. John 20:31, "But these are written . . ." Second, because only our belief in His
deity can prove eternal life (I John 5:1).

The truth of Christ's deity is not an academic
question to be argued as a theological or philosophical or biological proposition. It is the cornerstone of
Christian faith without which there can be neither
Christianity nor faith and certainly not eternal life
because unconditional eternal life is conditioned
upon our belief in the deity of Jesus Christ. The fact
of the deity of Christ is substantiated in history and
revelation.

In the Swiss Alps we met and talked with a Hindu
from Bombay, a sugar planter, who said to our
questioning of him about Jesus Christ, that in a few
hundred years Gandhi would be a god. In this fashion we have man-made gods. The real God is not
so made. Jesus was God when He was born. He was
Immanuel, God with us. (See Col. 1:15-17).

VI. An Inner Witness. 5:9-13.

Among the tests of physical life is consciousness.
I have a consciousness that I am alive. This consciousness is mysterious and in a sense mystical be-

cause I cannot identify it. I cannot cut out my consciousness and say here it is, but I know that I have such a consciousness and it tells me that I am alive. There is a spiritual consciousness as well as a physical and it tells us that we have eternal life. Like physical consciousness this spiritual consciousness is something mysterious and mystical but it is nonetheless real and demonstrable because it gives a commanding inner witness of our possession of eternal life.

The only authentic witness of eternal life that there is, is an inner witness. God doesn't authenticate our salvation through church councils or ecclesiastical systems. It is an individual matter and therefore it is an inner authentication and verification and every Christian has the witness "in himself." If you wish to find out whether you are a Christian find out within for "His Spirit beareth witness with our spirit that we are the children of God." In other words, you have the witness in yourself.

This inner witness brings:

1. Assurance of Salvation.

When you want to know whether a bill is paid where do you look? Well you can consult your feelings, but your feelings may be gratuitous and will always want all the bills paid and they may deceive you. You can consult your memory, but your memory may be faulty and it may fail you. Or you can consult the bill itself and if it is receipted or if you have a supporting check you know the bill is paid

and that paid and receipted bill is the witness in itself and it will satisfy your memory and stimulate
your feelings. (The Holy Spirit has receipted the
bill with His Sealing.)

2. Peace of Heart and Mind.

Lasting peace of heart and mind is the fruit of
having this inner witness for whoso has it has the
source of supreme Christian joy and happiness.
Peace is something from within and when the conditions of peace are fulfilled as they are in Christ, the
feelings of peace are abundantly evident.

3. Demonstrable Experience of Life.

Whoever has this inner witness has the basis for
an experience of life that can be without fear and
with power. In other words he will be able to dem-
onstrate what he believes by his life. And this leads
to the seventh and last test of eternal life.

VII. OUR LIFE. 2:29; 3:6-9; 5:18.

The character and quality of a life which possesses eternal life is that it partakes of the nature of
God and the chief characteristic of this life along
with truth and love is sinlessness. Therefore he who
has partaken of eternal life will live a life which is
marked by an absence of sin.

The great ideal for this life is stated in the second
purpose for the writing of this epistle, "These things
write I unto you, that ye sin not" (2:1). The ideal is
not that ye sin less or that ye sin least or that ye sin
some, but "that ye sin not." But then the apostle

goes on to admit the possibility of a Christian sinning by saying, "And *if* any man sin we have an advocate . . . and he is the propitiation for our sins." (2:1,2). How can "ye sin not" and yet sin? This troubles a great many people. It should be remembered that this question of sin among Christians was raised because of the presence of antinomianism in the early church. It was the mistaken idea that since grace delivered us from the law the believer is free from observing the obligations of the law and therefore could sin as he wished because God's grace covered all sin.

In 3:9 it says, "Whosoever is born of God doth not commit sin . . ." This means that sin is unnatural to the Christian because it is alien to his divine birth. Likewise in 5:18, "We know that whosoever is born of God sinneth not."

So we ask the question again, how can there be the great ideal "that ye sin not" in view of the fact that provision is already made for the possibility of a Christian sinning? How can there be this possibility of sin in a believer when God's Word says, "Whosoever is born of God doth not commit . . ." and "he cannot sin because he is born of God"?

The answer is in two directions.

1. In the Use of Language.

It is the difference between momentary acts of sin and continuous acts of sin. It is the difference between isolated acts of sin and sin as a practice. It is the difference between a single occurrence of sin and the habitual practice of sin. "Whosoever is born of God" does not practice sin although it is possible for him to commit momentary and isolated acts of sin, therefore "we have an advocate with the Father."

With this use of language in mind we read Scripture with understanding as follows: 2:1, "These things write I unto you *that ye do not commit an act of sin.* And if any man *commits momentary acts of sin* we have an advocate . . ." 3:6, "Whosoever abideth in him *doth not practice sin as a habit. . . .*" 3:8, "He that *practiceth sin in repeated and continued action* is of the devil. . . ." 3:9, "Whosoever is born of God *doth not practice sin or make it the habit of life. . . .*" 5:18, "We know that whosoever is born of God *does not go on sinning in continued and habitual action. . . .*"

2. In the Two Natures.

A Christian is a person possessing two natures—an old nature from his first birth and a new nature from his second birth. The old nature is the remnant of his Adamic creation while the new nature is the implantation of God's nature. Sin is impossible with the nature that comes from God because "his seed remaineth in him and he cannot sin because he is born of God." Whenever sin occurs in a believer it comes from his old nature and it comes from this old nature whenever the believer is not living a surrendered and yielded life. To keep from sin he must walk in the spirit and not in the flesh (Rom. 8). To keep from sin he must mortify his members which are upon the earth (Col. 3:5-11). But in any case the life of a possessor of eternal life will be free from habitual and practicing sin because that is the nature of God's life in us—to be without sin.

To illustrate this presence of the two natures we may turn to the orange ranches of Southern California. The famous California navel oranges were not always raised here. Originally California only raised seedlings which were small, sour and full of seeds. Years ago some trees were imported from Brazil. Cuttings were taken from these parent trees at Riverside and California orange trees were budded with these navel shoots and their character was completely changed. Instead of the original trees bearing oranges with seeds they bore fine new seedless fruit. But occasionally someone found fruit that grew out of the trunk from below the graft. It was from the old stock and consequently old fruit, small and full of seeds; and the only thing to do was to prune it or cut it off. But the characteristic of the budded tree was fine navel oranges with an occasional fruit from its old nature. The new nature produced new fruit and the old nature produced old fruit.

What was the answer to the problem? It was pruning or mortifying, cutting off, putting to death and self-judgment. Here is not only the explanation of the sin problem as it affects the Christian; here also is the effective manner in which to deal with it and live victorious over sin.

It is of the nature of eternal life to live without sin and in such a positive manner as to exhibit and display the characteristics of the divine life. High birth demands high bearing. Noble birth demands noble living.

These tests of eternal life are God's—they are the tests of God's Word. They are not the gratuitous statements of men who seek to confirm their own feelings. Happy are those people who can pass the tests.